HEART of GOLD

THE PEOPLE AND PLACES OF OTAGO

IAN DOUGHERTY

DUNEDIN TO DUNSTAN AND THE GOLDFIELDS

EXISLE PUBLISHING

NEW ZEALAND BEHIND THE POSTCARDS

Dedicated to the memory of David Dougherty senior, Marion Leitch, William and Elizabeth Hiscoke, Isabella Oliver, John Oliver, Bengt and Nilla Mattisson, Sigrid Mattisson, Francis and Mary McLean, Emma Webster, and James and Betsy Kitto, who sought a better life half a world away in a place called Otago.

(Above) **Curler in action at bonspiel, Idaburn Dam, Oturehua, Central Otago.**
(Front Cover) **For scarfies on the terrace at Carisbrook, there is nothing sweeter than the taste of an Otago victory over a visiting North Island rugby team.**
(Inside Front Cover) **Twins Doug and Des Appleby minding the store, Palmerston.**
(Right) **The Nugget Point lighthouse in the Catlins has been a beacon to shipping since 1870.** (Back Cover) **The moment of truth: a bungy jumper takes one giant leap from the historic 1880 Kawarau River suspension bridge near Queenstown.**

Copyright © 1998 Ian Murray Dougherty
Copyright © 1998 Exisle Publishing Ltd.
All rights reserved.

ISBN 0-908988-04-4

First published 1998
Exisle Publishing Ltd
PO Box 8077, Auckland,
New Zealand.
Ph: 64-9-303 3698. Fax: 64-9-309 0191.
e-mail: mail@exisle.co.nz
website: http://www.exisle.co.nz

Printed by Colorcraft Ltd, Hong Kong.
Artwork by Streamline Creative Ltd, Auckland.
Typeset in Berkeley and Frutiger.

Photographs by Jonathan Cameron, Chris McLennan, Denis Pagé, Gilbert van Reenen, Rod Morris, John King, Jean Gibson, Denis Todd, George Chance, Paddy Ryan, Ian Dougherty, Tim Chamberlain, Photosport, *Otago Daily Times* and Tourism Dunedin. Historical photographs: Hocken Library, Dunedin.

Designed by Raymond Salisbury, Heather Ball and C. Humberstone.

This book has been published in association with Wilson's Distillers, Dunedin, producers of New Zealand's favourite whisky. We gratefully acknowledge their support.

Acknowledgements:
For their generous help with this book thanks to Verdun Burgess, Roy Colbert, John Darby, Sue Edwards, Mat Ellison, Suzanne Ellison, Peter Entwisle, Charles and Jane Falconer, Lois Galer, George Griffiths, Bob and Janice Jones, Geoff Kearsley, Marie Keenan, Ron King, Alan Mark, Howard McGrouther, Murray McLachlan, Dave McLaren, John and Joyce Mullen, Chanel O'Brien and Tourism Dunedin, Michael O'Brien, Bill Parker, Tony Reay, Marshall Seifert, Michael Stedman, Grahame Sydney, Ian Taylor, Gary Tremain, Bob and Maureen Wood, and the crews of the *Earnslaw* and the Kingston Flyer.

FRONT COVER PHOTOGRAPH: PHOTOSPORT/RICHARD SPRANGER; INSIDE FRONT COVER & ABOVE: JONATHAN CAMERON PHOTOGRAPHY; OPPOSITE PAGE: DENIS PAGÉ, F/22 PHOTOGRAPHY; BACK COVER: CHRIS McLENNAN PHOTOGRAPHY; BACK COVER POEM: IAN DOUGHERTY; OTAGO TARTAN ON BACK COVER: COURTESY VILMA NELSON AND IVAN COWARD.

CONTENTS

PLACES

*"To discover this sort of landscape in your own country,
having been right around the world and ogled things that were
not half as spectacular, is really wonderful."*

– Garrick Tremain, painter, Wakatipu Basin.

(Above) **Lake Wakatipu, from the Remarkables Range.** (Right) **Rob Roy Glacier can be reached by an easy half-day walk from the Matukituki Valley, Mount Aspiring National Park.** (Opposite) **Mount Aspiring with the most common climbing route, the west/northwest ridge to the left, and the southwest ridge to the right.**

place which lies halfway between the Equator and the South Pole might be expected to possess a landscape and climate that were middle of the road, even wishy-washy. In Otago the opposite is the case. On either side of the straddled 45th parallel, the province packs into its one-eighth share of New Zealand's land area an unmatched variety of physical features and climatic extremes. Included are many of the nation's scenic icons.

In the north-west strut the alpine peaks and permanent snowfields which make up one end of the Southern Alps. These buckled mountains were formed by two enormous plates in the earth's crust being forced together along the Alpine Fault. To the long-term relief of Otago people, it's their Pacific plate which is coming out on top while the Indo-Australian plate to the west is going under.

Much of this uplifted land is encompassed by the 355,000-hectare Mount Aspiring National Park, which Otago shares with Westland. The park was established in 1964. Since 1990 it has also enjoyed UNESCO world heritage

status as part of the 2.6 million hectare South-West New Zealand World Heritage Area. Recognised as one of the world's outstanding natural heritage sites, it takes its place alongside features such as Mount Everest, the Grand Canyon and the Great Barrier Reef.

Otago's portion of the Mount Aspiring National Park includes the towering Mount Aspiring itself. At 3027 metres it is New Zealand's highest peak outside the Mount Cook region. To early Maori travellers it was Tititea or glistening peak. The name Aspiring was given by an early surveyor, John Thomson, who in 1857 hailed it as "a glorious pyramid of snow and ice". Some have stared in wonder and called it the Matterhorn of the Southern Alps. Others have climbed in exhaustion and dubbed it Mount Perspiring.

The first to sweat their way to the top were English army officer Bernard Head and a couple of local guides, Jack Clarke and Alec Graham, on 23 November 1909. Up to 100 climbers a year have followed suit. Some have died in the attempt.

Glaciers shaped Aspiring. There are still about 100 in the park. Even the largest, Bonar, Therma, Volta, are no match for the giant glaciers which bulldozed the huge trenches now occupied by Lakes Wakatipu, Wanaka and Hawea.

The Wakatipu Glacier gouged its way from the carved U-shaped Rees and Dart Valleys to Kingston, 130 kilometres away, and to 70 metres below sea level at its deepest point. Its legacy also includes the steep-sided mountain backdrop, the most dramatic example of which is the western face of the aptly named Remarkables. The Wanaka Glacier, which began in the Makarora Valley and was fed by glaciers from the Hawea and Matukituki Valleys, reached as far as Cromwell.

Within this glaciated terrain, early Maori discovered a treasure. At the head of Lake Wakatipu they found a type of nephrite or jade called pounamu or

greenstone. The area was second only to Arahura on the West Coast as the country's greatest source of the tough and beautiful semi-precious stone.

The Wakatipu greenstone was a pale milky-grey-green variety known locally as inaka, because it had a similar colouring to whitebait. It was softer than the dark green variety of nephrite and easier to fashion into weapons, tools and ornaments, before being hardened with fire.

The prime source of inaka was the long neglected Slip Stream area on the remote western side of the Dart Valley. In 1970 a deerstalker rediscovered the site, including a huge block of greenstone the size of a mini-bus and weighing more than 20 tonnes. It's the largest jade rock discovered in New Zealand and one of the largest known in the world. Understandably the site is now within a designated special area of the Mount Aspiring National Park and you need a permit to enter. Thankfully pub talk of planned raids with helicopters and explosives following the rediscovery has come to nothing.

To the east of the glacial lakes, the forces which shaped the Southern Alps were also responsible for Central Otago's characteristic parallel ranges and basins. They are unique in New Zealand and rare in the world. Sideways pressure caused a vast plateau of schist rock to break into a series of massive mountain blocks separated by wide flat valleys such as the Upper Clutha and Manuherikia. Among the mountains are the evocative Raggedly, Knobby, and Rock and Pillar Ranges and the Rough and North Rough Ridges.

Studded throughout this bare bones landscape are the craggy schist outcrops which make the place look like another planet. Leaning or Old Woman Rock

(Below) The Old Man Range is a stark and desolate area of Central Otago which has an eerie beauty of its own.

on the Dunstan Range and the Obelisk or Old Man Rock on the Old Man Range are the most impressive, the result of uneven weathering of schist of varying hardness.

These ranges and basins form the heart of the province. The snow-fed hydro-harnessed waters of the Waitaki River etch the traditional northern boundary. In the Waitaki Valley, thick horizontal beds of limestone have been weather-crafted into weird shapes. There's a good example near Duntroon where limestone outcrops resemble a herd of elephants ambling across a paddock. Nearby, the roof of a huge limestone cavern has collapsed, leaving a great canyon between two cliff faces.

Through the middle of the province flows the Clutha River, the country's largest by volume and second only to the Waikato in length. It too suffers premature aging at the Dunstan and Roxburgh hydro lakes before dissecting the rolling hills which buffer the inland plateau from the Pacific coast.

To the south lies the Catlins, made up of a series of parallel ridges and river valleys, again the result of more buckling of the earth's crust.

It wasn't buckling or glaciation, but volcanic activity which shaped Dunedin's hills and harbour, an ancient volcano later breached by the sea. These volcanic eruptions created Mount Cargill's soaring basalt columns known as the Organ Pipes. Similar columns can be seen at Lovers Leap on the Otago Peninsula and at nearby Blackhead.

An ancient undersea volcano was also responsible for the unusual lava flows at Oamaru's Cape Wanbrow. These include examples of pillow lava, or rounded

blobs of rock formed when molten lava was rapidly cooled by the sea water into which it was flowing.

The variety of landforms continues along the 530 kilometres of Otago's coastline, from the mouth of the Waitaki in the north, to the Brothers in the south.

On the Otago Peninsula and along the Catlins coast in particular, intimate coves alternate with wide estuaries, sweeping bays and sandy beaches. The most outstanding examples of the bays and beaches are Waipati Beach, Tahakopa Bay and Tautuku Bay in the Catlins.

Prominent headlands and cliffs towering up to 200 metres above the surging Pacific Ocean look out over reefs, rocky offshore islands and rock stacks. The most dramatic of the rock stacks are the vertically layered Nuggets at the end of the razorback ridge at Nugget Point.

Sea caves and blow-holes carved from the sedimentary rocks add the finishing touches. The Cathedral Caves at Waipati Beach are more than 30 metres high, while Jacks Blowhole near Jacks Bay is a 55-metre deep hole at the end of a subterranean cavern cut 100 metres inland.

The Catlins is also noted for its waterfalls, from the staircase Purakaunui Falls to the plunging McLean Falls at the head of a steep ravine on the Tautuku River.

The less spectacular North Otago coast has its own attractions. On a beach between Moeraki and Hampden lie the Moeraki Boulders. They look like they landed there from outer space. In Maori mythology they are the rounded food baskets washed ashore from the migration canoe, *Araiteuru*, which foundered

(Opposite Top) **The Moeraki Boulders at sunrise.** (Opposite Lower) **Snow tussock near the Lindis Pass.** (Below) **Purakaunui Falls, Catlins.** (Lower) **Reflections on Lake Wilkie, Catlins.** (Overleaf) **Sunset on The Nuggets, Catlins Coast.**

PAGES 9, 10-11: DENIS PAGÉ, F/22 PHOTOGRAPHY

in a storm and formed the reef extending out to sea from Shag Point. The scientific explanation is that they are the result of millions of years of accumulations of the mineral calcite.

The Moeraki Boulders are the best examples of their kind in the world, remarkable for their spherical shape, size and number. There are more than 50 complete boulders on the beach and others in the surrounding mudstone cliffs waiting to be exposed by the sea. Some are over two metres in diameter and weigh more than seven tonnes. There used to be more of the geological curiosities but they were preyed on by official and private souvenir hunters. Weight and legal protection are the saving grace of the remainder.

In Otago, landscape and climate go hand in hand, each helping to shape the other, and just as its landscape is the most varied, so its climate is the most extreme. The reason is simple. In the narrow island chain which makes up New Zealand, the most distance you can put between yourself and the temperate sea is 128 kilometres, and that puts you smack in the middle of Central Otago. Combined with the surrounding mountains which have the effect of both shelter and sponge it's far enough to give the area the closest New Zealand gets to a continental climate.

The Southern Alps are crucial in the process. Warm westerly air picks up moisture over the Tasman Sea, cools and condenses as it rises over the Alps, dumps its moisture in rain and snow, then warms as the dry air descends east of the mountains. The results are dramatic. Alexandra receives an average annual rainfall of about 350 millimetres or less than 14 inches. Across the Main Divide at the Homer Tunnel the average is around 7000 millimetres or 23 feet. At

(Below) **View of Karitane Beach.** (Lower) **Washed up krill on the Portobello shoreline, Otago Harbour.** (Opposite) **Catlins Coast, near The Nuggets.**

Milford Sound they have recorded more rainfall in 12 hours than Alexandra receives in 12 months.

Not surprisingly, Alexandra holds the national records for the fewest number of rainy days a year, at an average of 65, and the least rainfall over a 12-month period. Between November 1963 and October 1964 only 167 millimetres or about six inches of rain fell on the town. Alexandra also holds the national record for the lowest rainfall over a six-month period. While a depression covered the country's economic climate in 1930, in Alexandra they were crying out for a depression in the weather. Only 53 millimetres or about 2 inches of rainfall was recorded between March and August 1930. Nearby Clyde is the joint holder of the national title for the place with the lowest rainfall over a three-month period. Only 10 millimetres or less than half an inch fell between July and September 1966.

Not only is semi-arid Central Otago the driest place in the country, but in summer it is one of the warmest with day after day of hot dry weather and clear blue skies. Alexandra frequently tops the daily summer temperature charts and outclasses most places for sunshine hours.

There are warm dry pockets too in areas such as Strath Taieri, the home of the country's only inland salt lake. Thousands of years of evaporation from an enclosed basin has produced the Sutton Salt Lake with a salt concentration about half that of sea water.

Sutton's warm dry summers and sparse population also make the place ideal for nudists. Located about an hour's drive from Dunedin, the Orchard Sun Club continues to surprise and delight northern visitors with its brilliant weather. Club president Joyce Mullen is bemused by the reaction. People who start off by telling her she must be joking belonging to a sun club in the south, end up complaining not of freezing but of roasting.

Whereas Central's summers are dry and hot, in winter the temperatures plummet to produce the country's most extreme temperature variations. Ophir holds the official national record for the place with the greatest range of air temperatures ever recorded, at 56.8°C. This is helped by its top temperature of 35.2°C and the lowest official temperature ever recorded in New Zealand. On 3 July 1995 it reached -21.6°C. Ophir also held the previous record low of -19.7°C recorded on 2 July 1943.

Often the temperatures don't just drop for a day. In the winter of 1991 parts of inland Otago were frozen to a virtual standstill for several weeks. During the coldest winter in 60 years children went ice skating along the streets of black ice. Sheep lay down and were frozen to the ground. On the fast flowing Shotover River tourists who at other times would ride through Skippers Canyon in jetboats and rafts were able to walk from bank to bank for the first time anyone could remember. On the Arrow River four wheel drive vehicles made the 22 river crossings between Arrowtown and Macetown without submerging their tyres. A helicopter landed on the Lindis River.

The climatic extremes produce some seasonal oddities. Irrigation dams crowded with swimmers during the Central Otago summer double as ice skating rinks in winter. Clyde Dam construction workers had to add flaked ice and liquid nitrogen to water used in summer concrete pours. In winter they added boiling water and then had to insulate the newly poured concrete.

In defiance of the extremes, motorcyclists from throughout the country show

CHRIS McLENNAN PHOTOGRAPHY

BELOW: DENIS TODD

the right spirit. In the middle of summer they gather on the dusty delta at Twelve Mile Creek on the shores of Lake Wakatipu for the Remarkables Motorcycle Club's annual rally. The blistering Central sun is no place for leathers or tattoos, but they are undeterred. In the middle of winter the same hardy bikers pitch their tents in hoar-frosted paddocks near Oturehua for the annual Brass Monkey Motorcycle Rally.

In contrast to Central Otago, the coast is more temperate, with more middling temperatures and more moisture, and the further south you go the more moisture you get. North Otago's climate is closer to that experienced in Central Otago. In the Catlins it's more like the sodden West Coast.

For some outsiders, the word temperate is a euphemism for cold, damp and bleak, but that's not entirely fair. It's true that Dunedin doesn't rate well when it comes to sunshine hours and average temperatures, and it can have four seasons in a day when cold southerlies and warm northerlies alternate. On the other hand, it has fewer rainy days and less annual rainfall than both Wellington and Auckland. Besides, the official readings are taken at the Musselburgh sewage pumping station and as every Dunedin resident outside Musselburgh will tell you, it's the coldest, dullest place in the city. It's always much warmer and sunnier where they live.

(Top) **Winter scene on the golf course, Millbrook Resort, Arrowtown.** (Above) **The Brass Monkey Motorcycle Rally meets near Oturehua on Queen's Birthday weekend every year.** (Opposite) **Central Otago sheep farmers are hardy types used to the extremes of temperature common to this area. This Lowburn farmer and his dogs drive the flock down to a more sheltered spot.** (Overleaf) **Lake Wanaka from the popular walking track up Mount Roy.**

OVERLEAF: GILBERT VAN REENEN, CLEAN GREEN IMAGES
OPPOSITE: JEAN GIBSON

PLANTS

*"It's brilliant getting away in the bush for a few days.
Just brilliant. Although you can get a bit sick
of beech trees after a while."*

– John Harris, student, Dunedin.

(Above) **Wildflower bed, Central Otago.**
(Right) **Red beech forest, near Cascade
Saddle, Matukituki Valley.**

OTAGO'S varied landscape and climate have conspired to produce a huge range of vegetation, from the country's tallest tree to tiny flowers best viewed on hands and knees with a magnifying glass.

Gone are large tracts of the native bush which once covered much of the province, but there's still more than quarter of a million hectares left. Most of this is now protected within the Mount Aspiring National Park and the Catlins Coastal Rainforest Park.

Three members of the southern beech family tend to dominate. In the Mount Aspiring National Park, silver beech is most common, with red and mountain beech largely confined to the southern part of the park. Red beech, the tallest of the three species, prefer the warmer and more fertile lower altitudes. Away from the bushline they keep company with species such as the blood-red flowered southern rata.

The Catlins is a patch-quilt of silver beech trees, mixed kamahi and rata forests, and podocarps (native conifers), in places stretching from hilltop to coastline. The most common and impressive of the podocarps is rimu (red pine). You'll also find miro and Hall's totara, along with New Zealand's loftiest native, kahikatea (white pine), which favours swampy areas, and matai (black pine), which also prefers fertile sites but likes to keep its feet dry. The Catlins forms the largest remaining area of native bush and contains some of the last stands of podocarp forest on the South Island's east coast.

New Zealand's tallest single tree is not a native. It's a 70-metre tall Australian mountain ash, *Eucalyptus regnans,* in the Orokonui Scenic Reserve at Waitati. The tree is surrounded by similar specimens and is in such a sheltered position that it stands a chance of becoming the tallest tree in the Southern Hemisphere.

Beneath the Otago bush canopy flourishes a beauty and the beast world. The beauties include the white flowered native clematis and the crimson flowered mistletoe. Among the beasts are the perfectly named stinkwood, which pongs at the slightest touch, and bush lawyer, which won't let you go without trying to rip the shirt off your back.

The greatest variety of plants in Otago comes not in the trees, but much closer to the ground. In the Mount Aspiring National Park, the 100 metres between the uncanny spirit-level bush and snow lines contain one of the greatest ranges of alpine vegetation in the world. More than 90 percent of these plants are found only in New Zealand. The pick of the bunch (but they are protected so don't) is the world's largest buttercup, the great mountain buttercup, with its snow-white flowers and large round shiny leaves like green frisbees.

GILBERT VAN REENEN, CLEAN GREEN IMAGES

GILBERT VAN REENEN, CLEAN GREEN IMAGES

(Right) **Dunedin is known as the Rhododendron City.** (Below) **Kowhai flower near Lake Hawea.** (Lower) **New Zealand greenhood orchid, Makarora Valley.** (Opposite Top) **Russel lupins and Californian poppies near Johns Creek, Lake Hawea.** (Opposite Lower) **Mountain daisies, Harris Mountains.**

COURTESY TOURISM DUNEDIN

Otago's highest altitude plants are lichens. Among the permanent ice and snow well above the bushline they alone survive in snow-free nooks and crannies. Boggy alpine wetlands nurture a variety of small plants, including an insect-eating variety of sundew which traps the luckless insects in its sticky hairs and digests them.

Less sinister are the plants which thrive in the mountain-fed waters of Lake Wakatipu, the only large lake left in New Zealand to contain all of its indigenous and no introduced plants. The aquatic natives include one of the world's most outstanding collections of mosses and liverworts. The lake's exceptionally clear and pure water enables light to reach these plants at depths unknown elsewhere.

In the Catlins, the distinctive coastal vegetation includes the Nuggets daisy and Catlins forget-me-not which cling to the steep cliffs. The Otago Peninsula has its own variety of everlasting daisy. Restricted sites along the coast are home to the rare Cooks scurvy grass and the rare sand dune binding native sedge, pingao. Its golden orange leaves are important in Maori craftwork.

Central Otago is synonymous with tussock grasslands and cushion fields. At higher altitudes fescue tussocks are replaced by tall snow tussocks, and there's a wide expanse of tundra-like cushion fields on the highly exposed plateau summits.

Central's block mountains also act as botanical islands, containing plants and plant communities not just unique to Otago, but to particular mountain ranges in the region. Many have adapted to living in harsh saline conditions.

A good example is one of New Zealand's driest areas, Flat Top Hill between Alexandra and Roxburgh. Some of the country's smallest plants live here and several live nowhere else. These include wee spring annuals such as a native forget-me-not you can easily hide under a five cent piece. Its yellow flower is about the size of a pinhead.

Central Otago's other rare and tiny plants include a lepidium or type of cress which grows like a buried tree with leaves and tips of branches above ground, and trunk two metres or more underground. One of the three sub-species is down to a wild population of less than 100 plants growing on the sides of the Lower Manuherikia Valley.

Tall tree or tiny cress, Otago's native vegetation has taken a hammering over the past few hundred years. Plants which evolved over millions of years have been overwhelmed by axe, fire and the introduction of some aggressive exotic plants and animals.

In the Catlins, for example, 130 years of exploitation has reduced 130,000

GILBERT VAN REENEN, CLEAN GREEN IMAGES

(Above) **Spaniards, Ahuriri Valley.**
(Opposite Top) **Silver beech saplings in the rainforest on the bridle track, Makarora Valley.** (Opposite Lower) **Helicopter with monsoon bucket fighting scrub fire at The Neck, Lake Wanaka.**

hectares of native bush to 75,000 hectares. In an area where the pioneer frontier mentality continued long after it had been abandoned elsewhere, each felled tree represented another step in the march of progress.

The greatest number of trees were toppled in the 1950s and '60s. The clearance was driven by state-assisted farm development, the improved technology of chainsaw, bulldozer, tractor and cable-winch, and the shift from small-scale dairy to large-scale sheep farming. The most recent assault occurred in the 1980s when landowners and chipmillers conspired to clear as much as they could before official bans were imposed. By then, only 13,000 hectares of the original 68,000 hectares of native bush on private farmland remained in tact.

On the now largely treeless hills surrounding the Otago Harbour, the same economic imperatives prevailed. Slopes covered in trees down to the shoreline were turned into dairy pasture, the rocks into characteristic dry stone walls, as settlers got on with the job of earning a living in a strange land.

Less dramatic but no less damaging has been the effect of introduced animals. Deer, thar, chamois, wallabies, goats, pigs, possums, rabbits, hares, sheep and cattle have all eaten their way through the native vegetation.

In the Mount Aspiring National Park, red deer have been the worst offenders. Introduced as game to the Otago backblocks from the 1870s, they multiplied fast and spread far and wide. It was another century before commercial helicopter hunting and live deer capture drastically reduced their numbers, and their effects on the bush.

In Central Otago, rabbits have been even more destructive. It's reckoned that under ideal conditions, a pair of rabbits can multiply to a million in two years.

PAGES 23, 24-25: GILBERT VAN REENEN, CLEAN GREEN IMAGES

Central Otago was and is ideal. Introduced to the dry, predator-free interior as game in the 1860s, they turned vast areas to semi-desert. Rabbit-covered hillsides looked like they were on the move. With ten rabbits able to eat as much as a sheep, some runholders were forced off their land. At Earnscleugh Station the rabbits, welcomed as great sport by the first runholder William Fraser, ended up bankrupting him.

Something had to be done. In the 1880s the first rabbit board was established. Shooting was tried, initially on foot and decades later from motorbikes and helicopters. Predators were introduced, including stoats, ferrets, dogs and cats. One farmer imported more than 200 cats from Christchurch and released them on his sheep station. Wire netting fences were erected, traps set, burrows fumigated and flooded. Phosphorus-laced oats, strychnine and later carrots laced with 1080 poison were laid. Some rabbits responded by developing neophobia. They became bait-shy and refused to eat anything new.

In the 1950s the controversial myxomatosis virus was tried at Earnscleugh Station. The virus needed a carrier to transfer it from rabbit to rabbit, and mosquitoes didn't live up to expectations. The virus died out. The rabbits kept on multiplying.

The official rejection of pleas for myxomatosis to be tried again using fleas as carriers was followed by threats from desperate runholders to reintroduce it illegally. Attention then turned to another form of biological control, RCD, or rabbit calicivirus disease, which is claimed to result in a less horrendous death for the rabbits. This time the threats were carried through. The virus was illegally imported from Australia and released in Central Otago and elsewhere in 1997.

(Above) **Prince of Wales feathers ferns in rainforest, Makarora Valley.**
(Pages 24-25) **Red tussock near Lake Onslow.**

Long before the rabbits arrived, fires started by accident or design had destroyed much of Central Otago's former forest cover. Subsequent burn-offs, along with ploughing, topdressing, oversowing, and overgrazing, have worked hand in hand with the rabbits to take their toll on the tussock grasslands which replaced the forests. So too have the spread of exotics such as nassella tussock and self-sown conifers, particularly the fast spreading Douglas fir. More recently Central Otago has been invaded by the insidious hieracium or hawkweed.

One of the few native shrubs in Central Otago to survive the widespread burning has been matagouri or wild Irishman, its only redeeming feature a small white sweet-perfumed flower. As if the matagouri thorns weren't already large enough, agricultural fertilizer increased the size of plant and thorn. For good measure, European settlers added gorse, blackberry, hawthorn, thistle and sweet briar.

The ubiquitous sweep briar or rosehip bushes were brought in by gold miners as a ready source of vitamin C to prevent scurvy. The pink flowered briar is now the most widespread shrub in Central Otago. For generations of Otago youngsters it meant pocket money and scratched limbs. Both were collected while the small sweet red fruit or rose hips were picked for the manufacture of Robinsons Rosehip Syrup.

Other garden escapees include wild thyme. Introduced by the miners in the 1870s, it now covers thousands of hectares around Alexandra. During the 1930s commercial processing of the herb led to a thriving export industry. Today there's renewed interest in its claimed medicinal properties. Its aroma can turn an otherwise dour farmer into raptures as he explains the delights of driving a mob of sheep through a paddock of the stuff.

There are the more quirky exotics too, all reminders of the region's past. At the mining ghost towns in the Upper Shotover you can pick small sweet wild strawberries, and at Macetown, wild gooseberries. At the Goldfields Mining Centre in the Kawarau Gorge grows *Nicotiana rustica,* wild tobacco.

Continued assaults on Central Otago's tussock grasslands could be reduced by a proposed shake-up of land tenure covering 2.5 million hectares of South Island high country. The idea is to form new conservation parks from land

LEFT AND OVERLEAF: GILBERT VAN REENEN, CLEAN GREEN IMAGES

(Above) **Sunflowers near Mount Barker, Upper Clutha Valley.** (Overleaf) **Lombardy poplars near Beacon Point, Lake Wanaka.**

currently held by the Department of Conservation, land to be taken over by DoC with the phasing out of pastoral leases, and by covenants over freehold land.

Areas identified by DoC for new parks include the Old Man, Old Woman, Lammermoor, Rock and Pillar and Pisa Ranges, along with the Remarkables to the west. The aim would be to protect natural values, but also to provide for public recreation and limited commercial tourism. Pastoral lease land with farming potential and little or no conservation value would become freehold farmland.

The proposal has met with widespread suspicion. Conservation and recreation groups have expressed concerned over the commercial development of conservation land, the principle of the freeholding of publicly owned pastoral lease land, and on-going public access to and through it. Some farmers have branded it as another attempt by DoC to lock up further large tracts of what they regard as productive farmland.

Elsewhere, the pressure continues on other native plants. On the coast, pingao is under threat from the introduced marram grass. The fringes of some native forests are being smothered by old mans beard. Lagarosiphon, which was introduced as an aquarium plant, is smothering some waterways. It found its way into Lake Wanaka in 1972 and since then into the Clutha River and its Dunstan and Roxburgh hydro lakes.

The trend in Otago, as in other places, has been for trees to be replaced by pasture. There have been exceptions, though, and not just in the obvious planting of large-scale commercial pine plantations, farm shelter belts and garden trees. In Queenstown the once tussock-covered Peninsula was early on planted out in larches, eucalypts and Douglas fir trees. Part of Arrowtown's enduring appeal is in the main avenue lined with mature sycamores and oaks. Throughout Central Otago, long-established Lombardy poplars and willows help give the region its gilded autumn beauty.

PENGUINS PLUS

*"When we came here we just thought how lucky
can anyone be to have yellow-eyed penguins
living at their back gate."*

— *Janice Jones, honorary conservation officer, Moeraki.*

DENIS PAGÉ, F/22 PHOTOGRAPHY

(Above) **Hoiho, the yellow-eyed penguin, is easily distressed and should be observed at a discreet distance.** (Opposite) **Royal albatross with chick, Taiaroa Head.**

NATURAL variety in Otago is not restricted to the flora. The range of habitat has nurtured a similar variety of fauna, some rare, some endangered, some unique.

There's no better mainland site to see seals than Nugget Point. It has the largest mainland breeding colony of New Zealand fur seals. It is home to the only mainland breeding colony of southern elephant seals. And it's the only place where fur seals, elephant seals and rare sub-Antarctic Hooker's sea-lions co-exist. Leopard seals have also been known to haul themselves ashore for a rest.

Nugget Point has been earmarked as Otago's first marine reserve, in the face of opposition from many locals and cribbies who see the proposed reserve as a threat to their recreational fishing.

Otago is perhaps best known for its birds, and especially the yellow-eyed penguin (see Hoiho, pages 32-34). There are also several colonies of the more elusive but less exclusive little blue penguin. This smallest of penguin species is found throughout New Zealand and southern Australia. A few Fiordland crested penguins dot the coast. Occasional stragglers from several sub-Antarctic crested species, Snares, erect, rockhopper and royal penguins, come ashore to rest or moult.

Another well-known local identity is a relative newcomer to Otago. A colony of about 100 northern royal albatross has established itself on Taiaroa Head at the tip of the Otago Peninsula. With a wingspan of 3.5 metres, the world's largest seabird can stay aloft for days without a single wing beat, expertly using the wind currents to tack and glide above the ocean. Young birds initially head off for up to six years 'overseas experience' before returning to the windswept headland. Adult birds usually take a year out between breeding and do a complete circle of the globe via Cape Horn.

Taiaroa Head is the only place outside the main colony on the Chatham Islands where the northern royal albatross chooses to breed. Located 30 kilometres from downtown Dunedin, the colony also has the distinction of being the only mainland albatross breeding colony in the world.

Five species of shags (cormorants) share the province: black, pied and little shags, the cliff dwelling spotted shag and the rare Stewart Island shag, which is confined to southern New Zealand. One of the largest colonies of Stewart Island shags is at Taiaroa Head, where the robust birds nest on raised cups of tussock and guano at the foot of the cliffs.

One of The Nuggets rock stacks is the precarious home to a small Australasian

OPPOSITE: GEORGE CHANCE

HOIHO

THE BIG DIVER FROM DOWN UNDER

(Above) **The Yellow-eyed Penguin Trust helps raise awareness of this appealing bird and its fragile environment.** (Right) **Hoiho are best observed at dawn and the last few hours of daylight on their way to and from a day's fishing.**

IT'S a rare sight. A group of volunteers with spades over shoulders and flax bushes under arms, strolling across a paddock and singing, "Hoiho. Hoiho. It's off to work we go." The fun belies the seriousness of the task.

Hoiho (noise shouter) is the Maori name for the yellow-eyed penguin. To scientists they are *Megadyptes antipodes,* which roughly translates as the big diver from down under, so-named because of their ability to dive to depths of 100 metres or more in search of fish and squid.

The hoiho is found only in New Zealand, from Banks Peninsula to Campbell Island. The mainland birds, which are largely confined to the Otago coast, make up a genetically distinct breeding population. There is a second distinct population on the Auckland Islands and a third on Campbell Island.

In the 1980s it looked like the world's rarest penguin was about to go the way of the moa. By the late 1980s there were as few as 3000 yellow-eyed penguin left on the planet. More alarmingly, the total number of breeding pairs had fallen to as few as 900. The distinctive mainland population was down to fewer than 150 breeding pairs.

There were a number of reasons for the decline. Unlike most other penguin species which crowd together in noisy teeming colonies on bare rock, ice and snow, the modest hoiho prefers to nest out of sight of its neighbours. Traditionally this has been in the shade and shelter of dense, cool predator-free coastal forest. The search for a suitable nesting site might take a pair up to a kilometre inland.

On land, the loss of this traditional bush habitat to sheep and cattle pasture, and predation by stoats, ferrets, rats, cats, dogs and humans, had all taken their toll. At sea, the traditional foes of barracouta, seals, sharks and whales were reinforced by fishing nets, seasonal food shortages and a mystery disease which killed off parent birds.

The plight of the penguins galvanised the community. The efforts of groups such as DoC and Forest and Bird were bolstered by the formation in 1987 of the Dunedin-based Yellow-eyed Penguin Trust. It was funded by sub-scriptions, donations and an annual sponsorship from Mainland Products. The Dunedin firm had caught on that what was good for yellow-eyed penguins was great for cheese sales.

The work of scientists such as John Darby from the Otago Museum and individuals such as Bob and Janice Jones at Moeraki and Howard McGrouther on the Otago Peninsula was bolstered by hundreds of volunteers, from

(Above) **One of New Zealand's note-worthy birds.** (Below) **New Zealand Post featured hoiho and royal albatross on these 1996 issue stamps.**

schoolchildren to service club members. The hoiho became imprinted on the nation's consciousness and printed on the back of its $5 note.

As a result of the unprecedented community action, orphaned chicks have been hand-fed and sick and injured birds cared for. Reserves have been established, breeding areas fenced and planted in native shrubs, predators trapped and nesting boxes installed. Research and education programmes are being carried out. By the mid-1990s yellow-eyed penguin numbers had risen to about 4000, with the mainland population up to about 1000.

Those involved in the protection of the hoiho are passionate people, and passions have overflowed from time to time. The conservation effort has not been without its personality clashes and arguments over how best to ensure the survival of the birds.

There have been further set-backs too. In February 1995 fire swept through the largest mainland breeding area, at Forest and Bird's Te Rere Reserve in the Catlins. More than half of the reserve's 100 or so penguins were destroyed, along with the results of thousands of hours of work by volunteers in regenerating bush and trapping predators. Forest and Bird members immediately set about fundraising and replanting. If the yellow-eyed penguin is to survive, this practical approach by the locals will be one of the main reasons.

There are several small hoiho breeding areas you can visit along the Otago coast. Free public viewing hides are located at Bushy Beach near Oamaru, Katiki Point near the Moeraki lighthouse, Sandfly Bay on the Otago Peninsula and Roaring Bay near the lighthouse at Nugget Point. The Katiki Point site was developed by the Jones from sick and injured birds they have cared for since the couple retired to the former lighthouse keeper's residence in 1981.

There are also two private viewing areas on the Otago Peninsula. Southlight Wildlife offers self-guided tours. Local cocky Howard McGrouther's Penguin Place provides the best viewing, from a series of camouflaged trenches and hides within a few metres of nesting sites.

DENIS PAGÉ, F/22 PHOTOGRAPHY

gannet rookery. It has the distinction of being the southernmost breeding colony of the birds.

Otago's extensive wetlands, tidal lagoons and salt marshes support a host of waterfowl and waders. They also provide successive feeding grounds for national migratory birds such as the South Island pied oyster-catcher, and international migrants such as the eastern bar-tailed godwit, which makes its summer forays from Siberia.

Visitors who have taken up permanent residence along the Otago coast include the royal spoonbill. The birds established breeding colonies at Maukiekie Island near Moeraki and Green Island near Dunedin during the 1980s. The Australian migrants probably arrived via breeding colonies on the West Coast and in Marlborough.

Other ex-Aussie immigrants are the waxeye (silvereye), which arrived in Otago in the 1860s, the white-faced heron, the spur-winged plover and the stroppy white-backed magpie.

Away from the coast, the tiny rock wren spends its entire life above the bushline, nesting in crevices and feeding among the rocks and shrubs. Dwarfing the wren is another South Islander, the world's only alpine parrot, the inquisitive kea.

Otago's bush birds include a smaller relative of the kea, the South Island kaka, and a relative of the rock wren, the South Island rifleman. The hyperactive rifleman is the smallest of New Zealand's native birds. It keeps company with the grey warbler, brown creeper, tomtit, fantail, robin, morepork, wood pigeon, tui and bellbird.

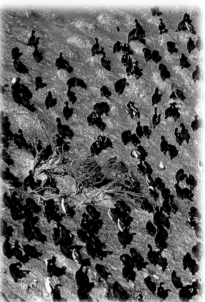

DENIS PAGÉ, F/22 PHOTOGRAPHY

(Top) **Black-browed mollymawk, Otago Harbour.** (Above) **Shag colony, Taiaroa Head.**

DENIS PAGÉ, F/22 PHOTOGRAPHY

(Top) **Jewelled gecko male, Otago Peninsula.** (Middle) **Alpine weta, Moutapu Island, Lake Wanaka.** (Lower) **Seahorse, Otago Harbour.** (Opposite Top) **Glass shrimp, Otago Harbour.** (Opposite Lower) **Juvenile Otago skink, Macraes Flat.**

(TOP): ROD MORRIS

(MIDDLE): GILBERT VAN REENEN, CLEAN GREEN IMAGES

Less common, to the point of being threatened, are the yellowhead or bush canary and the yellow-crowned parakeet. Both species were once widespread throughout the South Island but are now restricted to a few pockets.

In fast-flowing mountain streams and rivers the rare blue duck feeds on insects and vegetation. On lowland river beds the wrybill expertly uses its unique bent-to-the-right bill to search for food under river stones.

The large brown New Zealand harrier hawk wheels and dips above the tussock grasslands searching for food, or takes easier roadside pickings from that indiscriminate predator, the car. A rarer sight is the smaller, faster New Zealand falcon or bush hawk.

Less obvious but no less remarkable than Otago's birds are its insects. In Central Otago the range and basin landscape not only creates botanical, but entomological islands, each with its own species and communities. Moths, stoneflies, beetles, weta, caddis, cicadas and grasshoppers abound. New insect species are being discovered on a regular basis. Many are still to be named.

Otago's 3000 or so species of beetles include a unique species of flightless beetle which has evolved from a small population which became isolated in the Cromwell Basin. The Cromwell chafer beetle is a true Otago-ite, found only in a 95-hectare reserve of sandy flats south of Cromwell. This is one of the smallest known ranges of any insect in the world. First identified in 1904, the adult population of the nocturnal beetle had fallen to about 100 before the reserve was established in 1979.

Central Otago also has its own special lizards. Crevices in the large schist outcrops of two areas, the Lindis Pass and Macraes, are the last refuges for a couple of giant skinks. The attractive Otago and grand skinks, both shiny black with gold markings, are two of New Zealand's rarest lizards. Both are considered to be endangered.

The Otago Peninsula and the Waianakaurua Bush in East Otago are home to another rare member of the lizard family, the jewelled gecko. Its olive green tones with yellow or cream stripes on its back are not intended as a fashion statement. They are a very effective way of blending in with the trees and shrubs in which the lizards live.

Just as Otago's flora has taken a hammering over the past few hundred years, so too has its fauna. The loss of native habitat and the introduction of predators have been devastating for more than just the yellow-eyed penguin.

The Otago and grand skinks were once widespread throughout Central Otago. Loss of habitat to farming has confined their declining numbers to small isolated populations covering less than 10 per cent of their former range. Even the undemanding Cromwell chafer beetle has had its range reduced from 500 hectares to less than 100.

Predators were introduced in a saga reminiscent of the song about the old lady who swallowed a spider to catch a fly and ended up choking on a horse. Rabbits were brought in for food and sport. They became a pest. Stoats and ferrets were imported to deal to the rabbits. They ended up decimating native birds such as the yellowhead. Little owls imported from Germany to deal with introduced sparrows which were damaging Central Otago fruit crops also took a fancy to the native birds.

Fur seals, elephant seals and Hooker's sea-lions are making a comeback after being hunted to near extinction by human predators. It's a wonder the Hooker's

DENIS PAGÉ, F/22 PHOTOGRAPHY

ROD MORRIS

RYAN PHOTOGRAPHIC

GILBERT VAN REENEN, CLEAN GREEN IMAGES

sea-lions bother. The first recorded birth of a pup on the Otago coast in European times took place in 1993. Since then several of the rare mammals have been deliberately killed by guns, clubs or four wheel drive vehicles in the hands of idiots.

The northern royal albatross faced similar obstacles trying to establish a colony at Taiaroa Head. In 1914 they made their first recorded visit. In 1920 they made their first attempt to breed. A single egg was laid. One of the locals took it home for breakfast. Eggs laid in subsequent years were swooped on by collectors. In 1935 the first ever chick to hatch was killed by a dog. It wasn't until 1938 that the first chick flew from the headland. Stoats, ferrets and wild cats have continued to kill the chicks, despite on-going trapping.

An even higher price has been paid by some birds. Moa were hunted to extinction. The only kiwi left in Otago are in captivity. The kokako and red crowned parakeet haven't been seen for decades. The kakapo has gone not just from Otago but from the entire mainland.

ROD MORRIS

(Top) **The kea, the mischievous native mountain parrot, is usually seen above the bushline, but is attracted to human activity at lower altitudes.** (Above) **South Island robin in beech forest, Dart Valley.** (Above Right) **Himalayan thar are hunted on steep alpine terrain. This mature bull was photographed above Lake Wakatipu.** (Right) **Hooker's sea-lion pup, Otago Peninsula.** (Opposite) **Lobster krill washed up on shore, Otago Harbour.**

OPPOSITE AND LEFT: DENIS PAGÉ, F/22 PHOTOGRAPHY

PAST

"Otago may be bleak, and wet, and cold,
But what of that, when they've got lots of gold?"

– *From* The Lament Of Canterbury, *by J.M.T., 1862.*

(Above) **The Otakou Marae on the Otago Peninsula was built in the 1940s as a Treaty of Waitangi centennial project.**
(Opposite) **A fine example of neo-Classic architecture, the New Zealand Insurance Company building is one of many Dunedin buildings with an Historic Places Trust registration.**

POPULATION drift north, that trend which has been blamed for many southern ills, is fairly new in Otago. For most of the province's human history the population drift has been southward.

It began about 1000 years ago when the first wave of migrants landed from eastern Polynesia. Southern Maori traditions talk of Waitaha as the first arrivals in the 10th century. Then wielding the dual weapons of warfare and marriage came Kati Mamoe in the 16th century and Kai Tahu from about 1750, both via the east coast of the North Island.

The area was too cool for traditional Polynesian agriculture but there was enough to sustain a small population of hunter-gatherers. The search for food dictated fewer permanent pa sites and more kaika or seasonal settlements than further north. It also meant that by the time of the arrival of the fourth wave of migrants, Ka Takatapora or the shipboard people from western Europe, most of the land had already been explored and its features named.

Those names came to be expressed in a distinct southern dialect. For example, the standard Maori r sound was often spoken as an l sound. The north has its Waihora. Otago has its Waihola. The standard ng sound was spoken as k. The north has its Waitangi, Otago its Waitaki. Whitebait and pale greenstone were inaka not inanga, the people Kati Mamoe and Kai Tahu not Ngati Mamoe and Ngai Tahu, the newcomers Ka Takatapora not Nga Tangatapora.

Similarly, the standard k was often spoken as g. The name Otago, which came to be extended to the whole province, was not some clumsy European attempt to pronounce the name of the settlement of Otakou. It was an accurate phonetic rendition of the southern Maori pronunciation. To add to the confusion, the Maori name for the region is not Otago or Otakou, but *Araiteuru*, the name of the ancestral canoe which foundered at Shag Point.

The first of the shipboard people were captained by James Cook, who stayed offshore in 1770, naming Cape Saunders on the Otago Peninsula and writing of "a remarkable saddle hill laying near the shore". What's remarkable about Saddle Hill today is that such an historic and distinctive feature overlooking the Taieri Plain would be allowed to have the guts quarried out of it for road and airport construction.

After Cook came the sealers, the whalers and the real estate agents. In 1844, the Otago Block from Otago Harbour to Nugget Point was bought from local Kai Tahu chiefs. North and Central Otago were included in the Kemp Purchase, and South and West Otago in the Murihiku Purchase.

The Otago Purchase was the forerunner of an attempt to establish a distinctly

Scottish settlement, similar to those tried elsewhere in Canada's Eastern Ontario and Nova Scotia. For their village they mulled over various names, from New Reekie to Holyroodtown, and finally and thankfully settled on Dunedin, the old Gaelic name for Edinburgh.

A legacy of the two traditions, one Polynesian the other European, is an overwhelming number of Maori and Scottish place names and an unmatched number of names with a Scottish-Maori mix. Dunedin has its suburbs of Opoho and Wakari, Musselburgh and St Clair. The Maniototo, the Maori plain of blood, has its Scottish farmyard which includes Stotburn (steer creek), Gimmerburn (young ewe creek) and Kyeburn (cow creek). Places such as Strath Taieri take one word from each language. Gleniti does the same in the one word, combining the Scottish word for valley with the Maori word for small.

The Scots were a serious lot. They were serious about their Free Church of Scotland brand of religion, about the education of their children, and about building a settlement of substance. Creamy North Otago limestone, bluestone and brown breccia from Port Chalmers, dark grey andesite from the Leith Valley and red bricks from local clay gave them the building materials. The revival of Gothic and Classic forms of architecture gave them the style. Central Otago gold gave them the finance (see Gold, pages 50-55).

The result was an extraordinary collection of Victorian and Edwardian buildings. The best of them include Dunedin's Gothic revival First Presbyterian Church and Otago University Clock Tower building, the Italianate Municipal Chambers and the Flemish renaissance Railway Station. The private dwellings were just as impressive, among them Larnach Castle, the baronial mansion of

William Larnach, and Olveston, the Theomin family's Jacobean-style mansion.

Oamaru had a similar experience. Much of the town was built during rural boom times for North Otago wool and grain barons. Architects and stonemasons had a field day turning rural money and the high quality local limestone into architectural masterpieces. The best of them include the neo-Classic Bank of New South Wales (now the Forrester Gallery), the adjoining Bank of Otago (now the National Bank) and St Patrick's Basilica. They didn't stop at banks and churches. They took the same trouble over their warehouses and stores. The ornately carved Smith's grain store looks more like a work of art than a place to store wheat and barley.

Most Central Otago towns also owe their origins to gold, and their character to the dry climate and shortage of trees. Schist not only provided the region's geological building blocks, but the residential building blocks of its inhabitants. In the absence of timber, the settlers turned to the slabby schist for their houses and hotels, their barns and bridge piers, their fenceposts and stockyards. Schist was supplemented by sun-dried bricks made from local clay. The resulting buildings were well preserved in the dry climate, which was also kind to mining machinery and old mine workings. In the open Central Otago landscape, these not only remained, but stood out.

The building legacy can be seen in towns such as Clyde and Arrowtown which flourished. The building and mining legacy is evident in the relics of the gold mining ghost towns such as Bendigo and Macetown which were deserted when the gold ran out, but continue to haunt the landscape.

The discovery of huge quantities of gold turned Otago into New Zealand's

(Opposite) **Dunedin in 1870, looking north.** (Below) **Grand Hotel, Dunedin, in the 1890s.** (Overleaf) **Cardrona Hotel, a Central Otago landmark.**

Examples of neo-Classic and neo-Gothic architecture: (Right) **Dunedin Railway Station.** (Below) **Union Bank of Australia building, Oamaru.** (Lower) **Window detail, Otago University.** (Opposite Top) **St Pauls Cathedral, The Octagon, Dunedin.** (Opposite Lower) **Criterion Hotel building, Oamaru.**

most populated and prosperous province. It transformed Dunedin from a muddy village (nicknamed Mud-edin) into the country's largest and richest city, its commercial and industrial centre and its major port. It was the capital of New Zealand in all but name.

Outside Dunedin, an important place such as Palmerston at the start of the Pigroot to the goldfields was in no mood to be messed about by some tinpot North Island town. If the northern upstart wanted to call itself after the same British Prime Minister it would have to use the geographical qualification, Palmerston North. The small East Otago town still refuses to defer to the large North Island city despite the postal chaos.

One of the results of Dunedin's dominance is the astonishing number of leading New Zealand firms which had their roots in the city during the 1860s and '70s. Richard Hudson went from flogging off barrow loads of ships biscuits on the wharf to found the biscuit and chocolate firm which would become part of Cadbury Schweppes Hudson. William Gregg founded the company which would give the nation instant puddings and instant coffee and is today part of Cerebos Greggs.

James Speight and his partners founded what for a time was the country's largest brewery producing its most popular beer. Speights is now part of the Australasian brewing giant Lion Nathan, and the Otago working man's drink is making a comeback further north. The country's only legal whisky distillery, Wilson's Distillers, also traces its roots back to gold-boom Dunedin. The company which gave the nation's adults a rosy glow and its ungrateful children Maltexo is now part of Seagrams.

Henry Shacklock established the foundry which gave the nation's kitchens the Orion coal range and which would become part of Fisher and Paykel. Later, a young Scottish carpenter called James Fletcher arrived in Dunedin with a nailbag and a small bank deposit and began what would become part of the Fletcher Challenge empire. At Heriot in West Otago another Scotsman, Charles Todd, began the Todd family empire.

Socially too, Otago led the way. Karitane's Truby King gave the nation the Plunket system of child care. The world's first state social security system had its origins in a scheme to look after power project workers and their families in the Waitaki hydro town of Kurow.

The latter part of the 19th century belonged to Otago. The end of the gold dredging boom marked the start of relative decline as Otago grew more slowly than the north. During the 20th century, the province went from top-dog to

also-ran. Factories closed or moved north to be closer to their main markets. The city of the head office became the city of the branch office.

While northern cities were re-creating themselves in concrete, steel and glass, Dunedin's civic leaders were unkindly likened to museum caretakers. Otago went from a province of great builders to a province of great recyclers. It went from the most populous province to home for only five percent of the country's people. Dunedin slipped from the most populous city to seventh place and consoled itself with the knowledge that it was still the largest city by area.

Even Otago's boundaries weren't safe. Otago initially covered all of the South Island south of a line from the Waitaki River mouth to Big Bay on the West Coast. It subsequently lost ground to Southland, to Westland, and then to Canterbury. When the Local Government Commission was drawing regional council boundaries based on catchment areas in the late 1980s, half of the Waitaki District was lost to the Canterbury Regional Council. The Waitaki District Council and most of its ratepayers were not impressed. They continued to identify with Otago and celebrate its anniversary day and support its sporting teams.

A mining school shifting from one university to another wouldn't normally be expected to excite the general population. It was perhaps symbolic then of something much wider when in 1987 there was fierce public opposition to the transfer of the Otago University School of Mines to Auckland University. The loss of the mining school, which had opened at Otago in the gold-booming 1870s, came to symbolise the end of the province's golden weather.

But it's easy to overstate the case of Otago's decline and fall. After decades of privilege, it really only had the effect of putting the province on a par with most

(Top) **Andersons Bay Karitane Home, about 1915.** (Above) **Otago Boys High School.** (Above Right) **Campbell Park baronial mansion, Otekaieke, North Otago.** (Opposite Top) **Larnach Castle, Otago Peninsula.** (Opposite Lower) **Dunedin's Town Hall at night.**

other parts of the country. Still that didn't make the adjustment smart any less.

The exception to Otago's relative decline was and is the Queenstown-Lakes District, where tourism is the new gold. While the Waitaki, Central Otago and Clutha Districts continue to record population decreases and Dunedin only a slight increase, the Queenstown-Lakes District is the fastest growing territorial local authority in New Zealand. Queenstown and Wanaka have become the land of the mushrooming subdivision. Only Auckland city has higher average house sale prices.

GOLD

A RUSH OF GOOD FORTUNE

CHRIS McLENNAN PHOTOGRAPHY

(Right) **Chinese miners' village, Kawarau Gorge Mining Centre.** (Lower) **Visitor panning for gold at Kawarau Gorge Mining Centre.** (Opposite Right) **Last Chance Mine, Waterfall Park, near Lake Hayes.**

DENIS PAGÉ, F/22 PHOTOGRAPHY

G OLD had been found in Otago before the winter of 1861, but it was Gabriel Read's discovery near Lawrence of what he described as "gold shining like the stars in Orion on a dark and frosty night" that began New Zealand's first major gold rush.

Other discoveries quickly followed as news spread around the world and tens of thousands of miners descended on Central Otago. Horatio Hartley and Christopher Reilly took 40 kilograms of gold from the Clutha River near Cromwell and sparked the Dunstan rush. Bill Fox and his mates only succeeded for a short time in keeping secret their discovery of gold in the Arrow River. A couple of shearers, Thomas Arthur and Harry Redfern, found gold in the Shotover River during their day off. The Shotover would become the richest gold-bearing river in the world.

Initially, the miners took the easy alluvial gold which had been washed into the rivers. The recipe was simple. Take some gold-bearing gravel and water. Slosh them around a pan, or through a cradle or sluice box with slats across the bottom. The heavy gold will work its way to the bottom of the pan or be trapped between the slats. Collect a fortune. In an area desperately short of trees, timber was almost worth its weight in gold. By the time one runholder caught up with his missing dunny door it had already been turned into a mining cradle.

Away from the rivers, thousands of kilometres of gravity-fed water races were built across Central Otago to supply water for the large-scale high

DENIS TODD

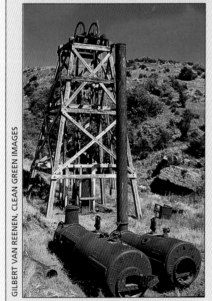

GILBERT VAN REENEN, CLEAN GREEN IMAGES

(Top) **Reflections of the past: Blue Lake at St Bathans.** (Above) **Poppet head and boilers at the Golden Progress Mine, Oturehua.**

pressure sluicing of hillsides. At Blue Spur near Gabriels Gully they pioneered hydraulic elevation. High pressure water was used to create a vacuum and suck gold-bearing gravel to the surface through a hole at the bottom of a long U-shaped pipe.

Next, the miners turned to hard rock mining in places such as Bendigo and Bullendale. They dug tunnels and shafts and used winches to bring quartz-bearing rock to the surface, where it was pulverised by stamps or hammers in deafening stamper batteries.

After a lull, the miners returned to the rivers and river flats and to dredging. Otago led the world in dredging technology, from humble beginnings with a leather scoop on the end of a pole worked from a pontoon, to huge mechanical monsters with a continuous chain of metal buckets. By 1900 there were 187 dredges clanking and groaning their way up and down the Clutha from the mouth to Lake Wanaka.

Gold mining in Central Otago attracted its share of dreamers and schemers. Several attempts were made to divert the Shotover River and work the dry river bed. The Oxenbridge family spent three years drilling and blasting a 230 metre long diversion tunnel through solid rock. They recovered only a pittance of the money they had invested in the scheme. An attempt to block off the Kawarau River at the outlet to Lake Wakatipu with a bridge and watertight gates resulted in a permanent bridge but very little else.

Gold is not just a part of Otago's pioneering past. In 1992, L & M Mining

HOCKEN LIBRARY, DUNEDIN

was dredging the Shotover, from where it's said to have recovered $26 million worth of gold in the previous year. Diggers with floating plants were also allowed one final go on the Clutha River before Lake Dunstan was filled.

After half a century of neglect, hard rock mining was revived in the Macraes area in 1990 when the Macraes Mining Company began operating at Round Hill. One of the largest open-cast gold mines in the Southern Hemisphere produces about a third of the country's gold output, all for export. Whole mountains are being moved to yield thousands of kilograms of gold each year from millions of tonnes of low grade ore. No one goes underground if they can help it these days. It's cheaper to rip off the overburden with heavy machinery than tunnel into the ground.

There are several smaller-scale mining ventures. At Island Block and Mata-kanui, shovels have turned into mechanical diggers, and gold pans into jigs and cyclones and knudson bowls. At places such as Kyeburn and Cardrona the job of removing larger stones by hand has been taken over by trommels, or rotating drum screens. Crude cradles and sluice boxes have turned into floating or land-based riffle boxes as the miners re-work old diggings.

Further down the scale come small suction dredges, with pumps and riffle boxes mounted on pontoons. Clad in wetsuits, the miners take hoses underwater to suck gold bearing gravel out of crevices. At the bottom end of the scale are the gold-panning hobbyists. About 20 people have $1000 hobby licences. Others do it illegally, and risk prosecution.

IN MEMORY
OF THE PIONEER GOLD MINERS
WHO PERISHED IN THE GREAT SNOW
1863

DENIS PAGÉ, F/22 PHOTOGRAPHY

(Top) **Scandinavian Sluicing Company gold claim at St Bathans, 1899.**
(Above) **Gold miners' memorial at Gorge Creek, near Alexandra.**

ILLUSTRIOUS ENERGY

RYAN PHOTOGRAPHIC

HOCKEN LIBRARY, DUNEDIN

There are also designated areas where you don't need a licence. At Arrowtown, for example, you can hire a pan and try your luck in the nearby Arrow River. At Winky's Museum in Skippers Canyon and the Goldfields Mining Centre in the Kawarau Gorge everything is supplied, including gravel.

In 1996, Otago extracted 4300 kilograms of gold, mostly from Macraes. At $22,000 per kilogram it was worth nearly $100 million. Chief Inspector of Mines Ron King says there's plenty left. He reckons there's probably as much gold in the ground as was ever taken out. It comes down to economics. At Macraes they still only extract 78 percent of the gold. The other 22 percent remains for new technologies to make the gold worth more than the cost of recovery.

(Top) **Miners' hut, Kawarau Gorge.** (Above) **Few Chinese people remained in the province when this famous photograph was taken in 1929.** (Opposite Page) **Scenes from *Illustrious Energy*, a 1988 feature film directed by Leon Narbey, which was set in Central Otago in 1894 and dealt with a small group of Chinese goldminers trying to scratch out a living from the barren hills three decades after the end of the goldrush.**

PROFESSIONS

"It never occurs to people here they can't do something.
They roll up their sleeves and get on with it."

– Michael Stedman, managing director, TVNZ Natural History, Dunedin.

I t's easy to think of Otago as one huge sheep paddock, when you drive along its country roads. There are about eight million sheep in the province, and another five million lambs, producing meat and hides, coarse wool for carpets and the finest high country Merino wool for fabrics.

Initially, wool was king. Old sheep were shorn, hit on the head and thrown into a pit or over a cliff, while Europe suffered food shortages. The key was refrigeration. In 1882 the sailing ship *Dunedin* left Port Chalmers for Britain with a shipment of frozen meat from the Totara Estate south of Oamaru. The carcasses were frozen on board the converted clipper for the three-month voyage. The same year, the country's first on-shore freezing works was established at Burnside near Dunedin. It was the start of an industry that would help sustain the New Zealand economy for nearly a century.

Otago also provided a new breed of sheep. At Corriedale in North Otago, James Little crossed the best wool and meat breeds to produce the Corriedale

sheep, with the dual virtues of long wool and prime carcass. The breed eventually spread around the world.

The Clutha district is one of the best sheep farming areas in the country, thanks to good soils, temperate climate, reliable rainfall and skilled people. Otago supports smaller numbers of beef and dairy cattle, with dairying prominent in the Lower Clutha and the Taieri Plain. These traditional pastoral activities have been supplemented in recent years by goat farming for meat, milk and mohair, and deer farming for venison and velvet.

At Clachanburn in the dry Maniototo, Charles and Jane Falconer have committed something of a local heresy. With the help of irrigation, they have diversified away from the traditional Maniototo sheep and cattle farm. Charles was sick of crutching and dagging footrotten and flyblown sheep. He dropped sheep numbers, deer fenced the sheep paddocks, and started breeding wapiti-elk deer. Some things don't change. As well as paying the regional council $10,000 a year for rabbit control, Charles spends another $5000 on helicopter and night shooting.

Meanwhile Jane has been diversifying too. She turned her hobbies into gardening tours and a cottage industry selling home-made preserves and handcrafts. She has also had a hand in publishing legendary Central Otago gardener Glad McArthur's *Lifetime of Gardening*. Generations of Otago people wouldn't do anything in the garden until Glad said it was the right time. She continued writing her weekly newspaper columns until her death in 1992, aged 87.

If a large part of Otago is a sheep paddock, then Central Otago is an orchard. Irrigated and free-draining soils in a dry climate, with hot summers and cold winters, help make it a major fruit growing area in New Zealand and one of the finest apricot growing districts in the world. The only drawback is blossom and

(Opposite Top) **Shearing time at Belmont Farm on the Otago Peninsula.** (Opposite Lower) **Rolling countryside, Hindon.** (Below) **One of the most significant events in New Zealand's history: the** *Dunedin* **leaves for Britain with the first cargo of frozen meat.**

JEAN GIBSON

OPPOSITE: JEAN GIBSON

(Top) **Roses are now
a blooming business in
Otago.** (Middle) **Cromwell has
its own distinctive welcome sign.** (Lower)
The pick of Central Otago's apricots.
(Opposite) **Central Otago cherries are
reputed to be the country's best.**

MIDDLE: DENIS PAGÉ, F/22 PHOTOGRAPHY

LOWER: IAN DOUGHERTY

fruit damage from late spring frosts, which orchardists fight with fire and water. Overnight they burn oil in frost pots or turn on overhead sprinklers to keep the frosts at bay.

Central Otago's 15,000 hectares of fruit trees and vines include 4300 hectares or more than half the country's area of apricots. The district produces about a third of the country's cherries and about a quarter of its nectarines. There are also large areas of apple orchard, plus smaller plantings of peaches, plums, pears, strawberries and grapes (see Wine, pages 60-61).

Complaints are not uncommon about the best quality fruit being exported. Most of it is. About 80 percent of apricot production goes to Australia, with smaller but important markets in North America and the Middle East.

Many South Islanders make an annual pilgrimage to Central to buy cheap fruit for preserving and jam making. Roadside stalls give excellent value for money, and pick-your-own (and eat-while-you-pick) is a popular and comfortable option for those with eyes smaller than their stomachs.

Central Otago's climate produces superb fruit. The climate and soils in other parts of the province make them ideal for timber production based on fast growing exotic trees. The versatile radiata pine and Douglas fir from the west coast of North America took to the wetter parts of Otago like the rabbits took to the drier areas.

Otago's 85,000 hectares of planted forest, including 65,000 hectares of radiata pine, is second only to the Central North Island in area. Based on even conservative estimates, the current output is due to double and then double again by 2020.

WINE

AN OLD INDUSTRY IN NEW BOTTLES

Wine making is one of those new Central Otago industries which has been around a long time. When the gold ran out, some miners didn't. They turned to horticulture and turned their mining races into irrigation races.

A French miner, Jean Desire Feraud, is credited as the first to do this commercially. From 1864 he used an old mining race to irrigate bone dry land on the outskirts of Clyde. Alongside his Monte Christo orchard of cherry, peach and apricot trees he planted a vineyard of several thousand cuttings imported from Australia and built a winery.

Feraud was elected Clyde's first mayor and went down in local folklore as Old Fraud because of what many regarded as shady deals over water rights. His name was mud, but his wines and cordials were the talk of the goldfields and beyond. They were dispatched throughout the colony and awarded prizes in Australia.

Grape growing and wine making never really caught on for a century after the so-called fraudulent Frenchman. The revival began in the mid-1970s when a few experimental vines were planted. They were initially regarded by most as a bit of a joke. People who had never heard of Feraud said it was too far south, too cold, to grow grapes in Otago. It wasn't until the 1980s that the latter day pioneers firmly established Central Otago as the world's southernmost commercial wine producing region.

The first commercial vintages were produced in 1987. By 1997 the fledgling industry supported 15 licensed wine producers on 150 hectares of productive vineyards, with more land being developed. It will never compete in size with northern regions but has already earned national and international wine awards.

Not that you can grow grapes everywhere in Central Otago, any more than you can grow them everywhere in European grape growing regions. Trial and error has selected a few sheltered, sunny, irrigated micro-climates, notably around Alexandra, Bannockburn, Gibbston, Queenstown, Wanaka and Lake Hayes. A similar micro-climate near Omarama in North Otago has allowed another vineyard to be developed there. Coincidentally, most of the sites have spectacular if somewhat unlikely locations, on terraces beside steep river gorges, on rocky hillsides, and beside picturesque lakes.

At Black Ridge in Conroys Gully near Alexandra, Verdun Burgess and Sue Edwards have established the world's southernmost vineyard and winery. Their 28,000 vines cover 6.5 hectares, with another couple of hectares still to be planted from their own nursery. After initially having their wine made

GILBERT VAN REENEN, CLEAN GREEN IMAGES

elsewhere, they now produce it for themselves and for other local vineyards.

The couple are typical of the spirit of the Central Otago wine industry, which is characterised by a down to earth approach and an absence of the pretension and snobbery often associated with the product elsewhere. Instead of turning an orchard into a vineyard, they started from scratch with a block of harsh dry rocky hillside which only supported rabbits, wild thyme and grass burnt brown by the summer heat.

Verdun, a former Invercargill carpenter, knew nothing about grapes until he bought the block of land in 1981. But the more he read, the more he became hooked. He took to grape growing with a passion, and to the rocks and the rabbits with a vengeance. Bulldozers and gelignite created pockets of land suitable for planting between the huge schist outcrops which couldn't be moved. A gun and eternal vigilance are the price of rabbit control.

For seven years Verdun and Sue held down fulltime jobs while they developed the block after work and at weekends. They lived in a caravan while Verdun was building the workshop, then in the workshop while he built the house. They didn't get their first return until 1988. Verdun now works fulltime at Black Ridge, where the couple employ two people and a winemaker and pickers as required. Sue's job in Alexandra continues to provide a regular income. The former Dunedin teacher also finds time to be president of the Central Otago Grape-growers and Winemakers Association.

From the Black Ridge vineyard, in the far distance you can almost see the remains of Jean Feraud's Monte Christo winery. It now bears a plaque honouring him as the father of the Central Otago wine industry. He might have been a fraud, but he was no fool.

(Above) **Rippon Vineyard and Ruby Island, Lake Wanaka.** (Opposite Top) **There can be fewer tasks more pleasant for a city dweller to contemplate than tending vines in the sunshine.** (Opposite Lower) **Alexandra's Black Ridge is one of the newer labels on the New Zealand wine scene.**

Most of the former state forests have been sold to Asian interests. The Malaysian and Singaporean company, Earnslaw One, bought the Conical Hills sawmill and state forests near Tapanui. Nearly half of the trees are still exported as logs, most bound for Asia, but further local processing is planned.

The mainly Chinese and Hong Kong-owned Wenita bought the Rosebank sawmill at Balclutha and the state forests at Berwick and coastal Otago. It plans a giant timber-processing plant producing sawn timber, veneer and fibreboard.

Offshore, fishing is big business. Most of the deep water fishing is carried out by trawlers chartered from Korea, Taiwan, Japan and Russia. The main species caught are squid, oreo dory, silver and blue warehou, hoki and ling.

About 85 smaller domestic vessels work the inshore waters from bases at Oamaru, Moeraki, Karitane, Otago Harbour, Taieri Mouth, Pounawea and The Nuggets. Their catch includes elephant fish, rig, shark, blue and red cod, flat fish, barracouta, groper, gurnard, stargazer and tarakihi. Crayfish (rock lobsters) are harvested with pots and paua by free diving.

The fleets at Moeraki, Karitane and Taieri Mouth sustain the seaside towns. Otago Harbour is the major service port and processing area. At Tirohanga near The Nuggets, the introduction of fish quotas has reduced the fleet to one vessel. In the absence of sheltered water, it still uses the traditional method of boats being pulled on and off the beach by a diesel-driven endless loop pulley.

Onshore, rabbit-prone land near Alexandra has been used for the country's first native freshwater crayfish farm. The freshwater koura are found only in the South Island, and are smaller and sweeter than their saltwater cousins.

Otago has a long history of turning water into power. The country's first

(Above) **Spillway at the Clyde Dam, Clutha Valley.** (Below) **Shark dissection for a public education programme, Portobello Marine Laboratory, Otago Peninsula.**

hydro-electric power scheme was not for some bright city. In 1886 hydro generated power was used to drive a quartz crushing plant at the mining town of Bullendale. The Dunedin City Council has been generating power on the Waipori River since 1904. Today water stored in the artificial Lake Mahinerangi is re-used at four small power stations on the river.

Mahinerangi is dwarfed by the lakes created on the Waitaki and Clutha Rivers. The Upper Waitaki has already been turned into a chain of hydro storage lakes, Waitaki, Aviemore and Benmore, with the possibility of a further dam on the lower stretches of the river below the Waitaki Dam. The Clutha is well on the way to the same fate. Having created Lake Roxburgh, and more recently Lake Dunstan behind the problem-plagued Clyde Dam, the power providers have shelved but not abandoned plans for a dam below Lake Roxburgh, at Tuapeka Mouth. Further dams above Lake Dunstan have also not been ruled out.

The locals pay a high price for the nation's cheap hydro-electric power. Lake Dunstan drowned Lowburn, part of Cromwell, 1400 hectares of productive land which included many of the country's best orchards, and the revered Cromwell Gorge. If the proposed Tuapeka Dam eventually goes ahead it will drown about 180 properties, including the town of Beaumont. It will also submerge 3000 hectares of productive farm and orchard land, 60 kilometres of recreational river, and native forests in the Rongahere Gorge. These include a rare example of unbrowsed bush on Birch Island.

At Nugget Point the protest signs read "No Reserves". At Beaumont they read "Reserves Not Reservoirs". It's a sentiment fully endorsed by Bob and Maureen Wood, who would stand to lose their best farmland and new home under 25

metres of water. Bob's people have been farming the land since the 1880s. Those who came before him are buried in the nearby flood threatened cemetery. Five generations on, the couple are determined to stay put. Power planners are not allowed over the cattle-stop.

Otago's primary industries support freezing works, cheese factories, milk treatment stations, textile mills and timber processing plants. Kaitangata in South Otago has a long established coal industry. Nearby Benhar once boasted the country's only toilet maker, McSkimmings, until the lid was lifted on imports, and the industry itself went down the toilet.

Despite its rural reputation, nearly two-thirds of Otago's population of 190,000 live in Dunedin. The province has more clerks and more factory workers than farm and forestry workers.

Dunedin's biggest industry is education. In a city of 120,000, about 15,000 or one in eight are Otago University students. About 70 percent of the students come from out of town and live in halls of residence and student flats within walking distance of the campus and the city centre. The university is also a major employer, with an equivalent fulltime staff of 1800.

The students and staff are attracted by the university's reputation for quality education and laid-back campus lifestyle. Otago is also the only New Zealand university to offer degree courses in pharmacy, dentistry, surveying, physical education and consumer and applied sciences.

The country's oldest university shares an expanded North Dunedin campus with the oldest teachers' college, now called the Dunedin College of Education, and the Otago Polytechnic.

RYAN PHOTOGRAPHIC

(Above) **Sheep farming has been a staple of the Otago economy for well over a century.** (Below) **The Robinson bell foundry, Dunedin.**

DENIS PAGÉ, F/22 PHOTOGRAPHY

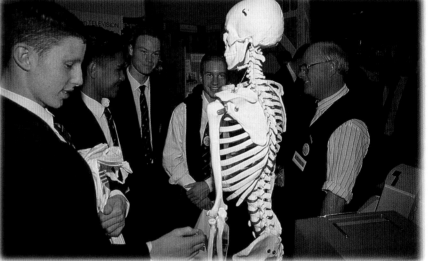

(Top) **Winter scene on campus near the Clock Tower building, Otago University.** (Above Right) **Students at a careers exhibition.** (Above) **Otago University's courses are marketed well and attract students from throughout New Zealand and overseas.**

The College of Education has about 1000 full or part-time students, most training for early childhood and primary teaching while also attending the university. The Otago Polytechnic has more than 9000 full or part-time students in Dunedin and at regional campuses in Oamaru, Cromwell and Queenstown. Near Balclutha, the smaller Telford Rural Polytechnic offers a variety of land-based courses from agriculture to beekeeping.

As well as education, Dunedin's salvation is seen in tourism (discussed later) and niche marketing. Away from the main markets in a deregulated world, Dunedin people have realised they can no longer compete in fields such as large-scale engineering, and have turned instead to more specialist areas. Television computer graphics, for example, have been pioneered in Dunedin in a joint project by a local television production company and the university (see Animation, pages 68-69).

Dunedin is also home to the acclaimed TVNZ Natural History, which has grown from cottage industry into the world's third-largest producer of natural history television programmes. The flagship *Wild South* programmes alone have been watched by an estimated 180 million people in 130 countries, and have won more than 100 international awards at every major film and telelvision festival.

TVNZ Natural History has also worked on productions in partnership with the BBC, the Discovery Channel, National Geographic, Turner Broadcasting, PBS and other leading public and private television production companies around the world. On-going projects include a major 10-part series called *Wild Asia,* being made in tandem with Japan's national broadcaster NHK.

The Natural History crews have filmed in some of the most extreme environments in the world, from the blast furnaces of deserts to the blood-chilling

(Top) **Demonstration of electron microscope, Otago School of Medicine.** (Above Left) **Biochemistry students, Otago University.** (Above) **Dunedin's Public Art Gallery is one of the country's most dynamic, exhibiting the finest art from New Zealand and around the world, including the record-breaking Masterpieces From The Guggenheim Museum exhibition in 1997.**

ANIMATION

Mention the word animation and most people would probably think Disney and Hollywood. Even in a computer age where geographical remoteness is no barrier to technological sophistication, Dunedin still seems an unlikely place to have pioneered computer animation. But as former television presenter Ian Taylor asked himself, why not? The technocrats of California might have confidence to burn, but they don't have a monopoly on creativity and few would share the do-it-yourself versatility of New Zealanders.

Animation Research Ltd was set up in 1989, initially as a joint venture between local television production company Taylormade Productions and the University of Otago Computer Sciences Division, whose graphics department was conducting research into 3D computer modelling. Ian Taylor saw the potential and proposed combining the academic with the practical, forming Animation Research Ltd to explore the opportunities.

Dunedin being a relatively small, close-knit community meant that the venture was established on a handshake. Ian Taylor points out that this lack of formality was important, because at first they were not exactly flooded with work. The New Zealand television and advertising industries looked to the United States for this type of technology. Even if the decision-makers had been aware of what was going on 'down south', few would have given credence to a small group of enthusiasts being capable of achieving similar results to the big computer graphics companies of New York and Los Angeles.

Ironically, ARL's breakthrough came with a television commercial for Chicago-based United Airlines. The images were totally computer-generated and featured a United 747 flying over Paris, the Grand Canyon, Rio de Janeiro and Hawaii. It was the first television commercial the Dunedin company had produced, and it won awards around the world.

The next major achievement came in 1991 with the development of the America's Cup software (although by this time the university was no longer involved). Created in just six weeks, the animation program had an enormous impact on the way people saw the event. The tricky geometry of yacht racing suddenly was made understandable to people who didn't know a jib from a genoa. For the first time, television viewers were able to see exactly what was happening out on the water (and under it too), who was in front and by how much. It was television at its best. Such was the impact of these animations that it is hard to imagine America's Cup coverage in the future without this package, or a development of it.

ARL's programmers are an ingenious lot. They can turn a plain old one-

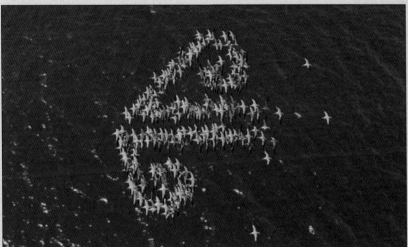

GRAPHICS COURTESY ANIMATION RESEARCH LTD

dimensional topo map of Mount Everest into a super-realistic airborne sequence which takes the viewer zooming above the icefield towards the summit. You can even see snow blowing off the peak. They have combined their ingenuity with a quirky sense of humour to produce outstanding work such as the Bluebird skiing penguin commercial. The best of their animations also have the power to evoke deeper emotions, as in their celebrated Air New Zealand commercial, where gannets flock to form the koru.

Expensive off-the-shelf animation packages are nowhere near sophisticated enough for what ARL requires. The company has diversified into developing software which translates actual movements of people into lifelike actions of animated characters. Art imitating life, literally. One example can be seen at the Museum of New Zealand in Wellington, which features a computer-generated character called Rima who acts as a guide for its 'Future Zone'. Rima took ARL only four months to develop, at a fraction of the time and cost it's estimated would be necessary if this had been commissioned overseas.

"We write our own software here," Ian Taylor says matter-of-factly, and only because you ask. It's a very Otago attitude. Why not go for the best in the world? Why not go for gold?

(Above, and Opposite Page) Graphic frames from the America's Cup race sequences, which helped put Dunedin's Animation Research Ltd on the map. (Top) ARL's Bluebird penguin commercial. (Above Left) The gannet sequence for Air New Zealand.

COURTESY TVNZ NATURAL HISTORY/JEANIE ACKLEY

waters beneath the Antarctic pack-ice. Their underwater camera work in particular is regarded as being second to none, thanks to the expertise of the divers and the use of their own purpose-built Remote Operated Vehicle, which can film at depths of more than 600 metres.

When television bosses wanted to move the unit north, managing director Michael Stedman told them they could shift the equipment in two truckloads and do the job from anywhere in the world, it didn't matter. What mattered was the people and they chose to live in Dunedin. They stayed put.

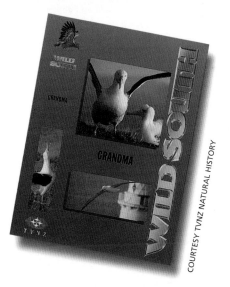

COURTESY TVNZ NATURAL HISTORY

(Top) **TVNZ Natural History cameraman Peter Thompson diving with southern right whales in Port Ross, Auckland Islands for the *Wild South* documentary *The Lost Whales*. (Opposite) Bill Dooley is a master stonemason who specialises in Oamaru stone.**

OPPOSITE: JONATHAN CAMERON PHOTOGRAPHY

PLEASURES

"I am one of those regionalists who are saying here's where I live on the earth and here's what I love. I never feel like working when I'm anywhere else."

– Grahame Sydney, painter, Dunedin.

SPORT has always played a major part in the life of Otago. It produces some of the country's very best sports people. Jean Stewart and Danyon Loader in swimming, athletes Yvette Williams and Harold Tyrie, Bert Sutcliffe in cricket, the Turner brothers who have each represented New Zealand, Brian in hockey, Glen in cricket and Greg in golf. Otago people are quick to point out it was on Otago Harbour as a schoolboy that America's Cup skipper Russell Coutts learned how to sail.

Above all, Otago has produced some of the country's greatest rugby players. Talk to rugby historians and they will speak fondly of the legendary Jack Taiaroa, the first Maori to play rugby for New Zealand. After Taiaroa came players of the calibre of Jock Richardson, Ron Elvidge, Kevin Skinner, Peter Johnstone, and player-coaches Jimmy Duncan and Charlie Saxton. Other contributions to the national game include the All Black uniform of black shirt and silver fern, suggested by Otago-born Tom Ellison, who captained the first official New Zealand rugby team.

(Below) **1996 Olympic double-gold medallist Danyon Loader at an emotional homecoming in the Octagon with the chef de mission Dave Gerrard and coach Duncan Laing. (Opposite) Danyon Loader training at Moana Pool, Dunedin.**

(Top) **Vincent County rugby football team, 1906. "Premier county team of Otago. Points for, 91, Against 3". (Above) Score-board at Carisbrook, the famed 'House of Pain'. (Previous Page) Carisbrook, the home of Otago rugby, is renown for its atmosphere which is unmatched anywhere in New Zealand.**

Large doses of sporting pride are injected into the Otago rugby team, through good times and bad. After three decades of trying, Otago won the Ranfurly Shield in 1935. With Southland it kept the shield south of the Waitaki River until 1950, and held it again briefly in 1957.

The low point in Otago rugby, and in the lives of many of its supporters, was 1979 when the team came within a missed opposition penalty kick (from in front of the posts) of relegation to the second division. The near shame was replaced by jubilation in 1991 when Otago took the national championship for the first time. In 1994 adults openly wept on the terraces and in the stands when a successful last minute opposition penalty prevented Otago from taking the Ranfurly Shield for the first time since 1957.

Carisbrook, the home of Otago rugby and cricket, is as much shrine and sacrificial altar as sporting ground. Affectionately known by the locals as the Brook, defeated visiting rugby teams have dubbed it the House of Pain.

Carisbrook crowds are often large and always opinionated. A total of 41,500 people turned up to watch the first rugby test between New Zealand and South Africa in 1994. Otago wasn't playing so they supported New Zealand. Traditionally the crowd has always been larger than the official figures. These never included the Scotsman's Grandstand on the railway embankment overlooking the ground. Much to the displeasure of its former non-paying patrons, the area has finally been fenced off.

One tradition which continues at Carisbrook involves the Otago University students, or scarfies as they are called because of their scarves in Otago colours of blue and gold. Particularly during the cricket season, sofas from their student

flats become 'hospitality suites' on the terraces. The students are not just well represented in the crowds. The Otago University rugby club has produced more All Blacks than any other club in the country, well ahead of the second ranked Ponsonby club in Auckland. Whereas the population drift north has eroded rugby's traditional southern power base, in Otago this has been partly offset by players drifting south to attend Otago University and then staying on in Dunedin.

The university has also helped foster other worthy pursuits in the province through its three fellowships, Frances Hodgkins in art, Robert Burns in writing and Mozart in music. Each has brought people from outside the province for a year to complement the local talent. Some of the visitors, such as Hodgkins Fellows Ralph Hotere and Marilynn Webb, have stayed on.

Otago's rich art history dates back several centuries. The earliest artists worked with campfire charcoal, animal fat and volcanic red ochre on rock. Their stylised images can still be seen on the limestone shelters they used while travelling through North Otago and South Canterbury. Not the best but certainly the most accessible of the early Maori rock drawings are at Takiroa and Maraewhenua near Duntroon.

For early European painters, Paradise at the head of Lake Wakatipu had nothing to do with the paradise ducks after which it was named. It and the whole Wakatipu region really were Paradise. The area inspired early surveyor-painters such as John Thomson, John Buchanan and Charles Kettle. Later it had the same effect on William Hodgkins, father of Fanny and largely responsible for starting the Dunedin Public Art Gallery, the country's first.

Charles Blomfield walked to the southern lakes from Mount Cook with

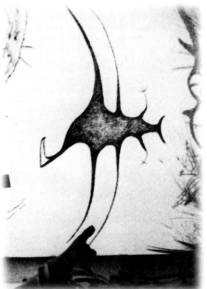

(Top) **Artist Ralph Hotere at his Careys Bay home, 1979.** (Above) **Ancient Maori rock art depicting a stylised bird, Oamaru district.**

(Right) **Hone Tuwhare has been a leading New Zealand poet since the 1960s.** (Below) **Many of Janet Frame's fictional settings evoke a distant but recognisable Otago.** (Lower) **Colin McCahon was influenced by the light and landforms of his province.** (Opposite Top) **The Burton Brothers left an invaluable legacy of 19th century images of Otago, including this self-portrait.** (Opposite Middle) **Poet James K. Baxter as a young man of 18.** (Opposite Lower) **Prolific publisher and writer A.H. Reed on the road at 88, March 1964, nearing the end of one of his many endurance epics.**

canvases strapped to his back to paint the scenic splendours of the region. Nicholas Chevalier arrived in style with attendants and in the pay of the Otago Provincial Government to do the same. James Richmond, John Gully, Laurence Wilson, William Fox, George O'Brien and John Hoyte were similarly gob-smacked by the grandeur.

As well as inspiring outsiders, Otago nurtured arguably the country's two greatest painters, Fanny Hodgkins and Colin McCahon. The inspiration for Colin McCahon was more mystical than real. He claimed to have gazed over the Taieri Plain and seen what he called an angel, or a new way of looking at the land, which he then tried to paint.

The landscape has more recently inspired Michael Smither, Robin White, Marilynn Webb, who was drawn to the Lake Mahinerangi area, and Grahame Sydney, who became obsessed with the landscape of Central Otago.

Dunedin-born Grahame Sydney went to London in the early 1970s and started dreaming about Central Otago. They were dreams full of wide, desolate Central Otago valleys and gigantic skies. The images haunted him and he returned home to paint them. The former Hodgkins Fellow talks of the solitude and the stillness of Central Otago and the pathetic attempts people have made to try to be important and permanent when they are neither.

At the same time, the more scenic tradition of landscape painting begun by Douglas Badcock and Peter McIntyre has been continued by painters such as Brain Halliday, Graham Brinsley, Neil Bartlett and Garrick Tremain.

More widely known as an award-winning cartoonist, North Islander Gary Tremain shifted to the Wakatipu Basin in the early 1970s looking for a better lifestyle. What he found was a stunning climate, and a landscape that knocked his eyes out. He talks of the size and power and detail and beauty of the landscape and the magic of the winter light. People tell him he's very lucky to live where he does. He tells them he's very wise to live there.

The landscape has been a magnet too for photographers such as Alfred Burton of Dunedin's famous Burton brothers. The roving photographer with his horse-drawn darkroom achieved a worldwide reputation for his views of the region and helped make it a popular resort for visitors. George Moodie, who took over

the Burton brothers' business, also popularised the region with his scenic postcards. Many of the photographs of Lake Wakatipu taken in the 1880s by freelance photographer F. Muir are ranked by local photography historian Hardwicke Knight as among the finest examples of landscape photography in the world.

More recently film and television crews from around the world have been drawn by Central Otago's landscape, dry climate and clear skies. The movies have ranged from *Illustrious Energy,* about the experiences of Chinese goldminers in Central Otago, to the medieval fantasy *Willow* and the adventure film *Race For The Yankee Zephyr.*

The landscape has also played an important part in Otago's strong literary tradition. It has inspired poets, from the country's first half-decent poet, immigrant John Barr, and his fellow import Thomas Bracken, to local boys Charles Brasch and James K. Baxter. Born and raised at Brighton near Dunedin, Jimmy Baxter later wrote that more than half of the images that recur in his poems were connected with memories of the township and its river, hills and sea-coast.

Denis Glover and writer-politician John A. Lee were both born and raised in Dunedin. Janet Frame was Dunedin-born, Oamaru-bred. Both places pop up by name or alias in her writings. The Central Otago landscape and its rural way of life have provided a rich source of material for the prolific Ross McMillan, the Naseby farmer better known to his many admirers as Blue Jeans.

Jimmy Baxter and Janet Frame were both Burns Fellows at Otago University. So too have been the likes of outsiders Maurice Shadbolt, Maurice Gee, Hone Tuwhare, Sam Hunt, Keri Hume, Roger Hall and Owen Marshall.

The proud literary tradition extends to publishing. In Dunedin, Alfred Reed founded the publishing firm AH & AW Reed, and donated his priceless collection of rare books to the people of the city. Books and paintings collected by local doctor Tom Hocken formed the basis of the major historical research library and art collection named after him. The firm of John McIndoe has been a major publisher of New Zealand books. Otago Heritage Books unashamedly specialises in regional book publishing and selling.

Not only does the province have a rich history, but the most and the fattest

history books. When the province in 1948 celebrated the 100th anniversary of the Otago settlement, the locals couldn't think of a better way to mark the occasion than by adding a couple of dozen more Otago history books to the pile.

It seems appropriate then that Dunedin should be the city to host Wordstruck, which brings together writers from New Zealand and overseas every second year for a week-long festival. The city which holds a writers' week also features a writers' walk. A series of pithy writers' quotes about Dunedin have been immortalised in bronze plaques embedded in the footpath around the Octagon at the heart of the city.

The Octagon is also the place where queues form each June for the Regent Theatre's 24-hour fundraising book sale. The country's biggest second-hand book sale is a mark both of Otago people's generosity and their fondness for reading. Several hundred thousand books are donated and sold each year in the fundraising marathon. The south also chalks up the country's highest rate of new book sales per head of population. This has been unkindly explained by some as more a reflection of the weather than the thirst for knowledge.

The province which gave the All Blacks their national uniform also gave the country its national anthem, *God Defend New Zealand*. Dunedin journalist, poet and politician Tom Bracken wrote the words and then ran a competition to set them to music. Lawrence schoolteacher and later county clerk John Woods obliged by knocking out the tune in a single sitting. The talented musician was able to play the tune on 11 different musical instruments.

(Above) **Otago has a keen sense of its history, which is chronicled in numerous books.** (Below) **Playwright Roger Hall with an enthusiastic audience of young book lovers during the Wordstruck festival.**

A century later came another of Otago's claims to musical fame, the Dunedin Sound. The label has been given to bands which came out of the city from the late 1970s, among them the Enemy, followed by the Chills, the Bats, the Verlaines, the Clean, Straitjacket Fits and the 3Ds.

The Dunedin Sound is not a label the black-clothed band members have happily worn themselves. It's been applied to them by others for their roughly similar sound based on strong original songs, often performed with jangling guitars drowning out the mournful vocals.

The music is also characterised by a contempt both for outside trends and for a polished studio production sound. Auckland bands might rehearse for months before they went on stage. The Dunedin bands would get up at a local pub, the Empire, the Crown, the Oriental, and perform a song with the freshly written lyrics taped to a microphone stand.

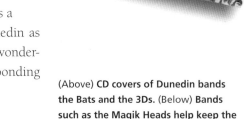

At home the bands have been hugely underrated. Martin Phillipps and the Chills have made the widest impact, getting to number one in the album charts, number two in the singles charts, filling the Dunedin Town Hall and being honoured with a mayoral reception at the end of a world tour.

Overseas, the Dunedin Sound has been hailed by rock journalists as a major musical movement. The *Chicago Sun-Times* has described Dunedin as the Liverpool of the 1990s. Such comments have left many of the bands wondering why this international fame has not been accompanied by a corresponding fortune.

(Above) **CD covers of Dunedin bands the Bats and the 3Ds. (Below) Bands such as the Magik Heads help keep the 'alternative' Dunedin Sound alive.**

PLAY

*"At the odd time we thought we'd try somewhere else,
but we always ended up back here. The mountains
and the lake and fishing. It's so special."*

– *Bill Parker, holidaymaker, Glendhu Bay.*

(Above) **Bungy jumping has become a
multi-million dollar tourism drawcard.**
(Right) **A lone hang glider pilot plays the
winds off Allans Beach, Otago Peninsula.**
(Overleaf, pages 84-85) **1996 Warbirds Over
Wanaka airshow display.** (Top, page 86)
Grumman TBF Avenger over Lake Wanaka.
(Lower, page 86) **The mountain bike
section of the annual Ghost to Ghost
Triathlon above Blue Lake, St Bathans.** (Far
Right, page 87) **Another brave tourist takes
the plunge off the Skippers Canyon
suspension bridge, 71 metres above the
Shotover River.**

ABOVE: DENIS PAGÉ, F/22 PHOTOGRAPHY
PAGES 84–85: JOHN KING

*Has gained all touch of reality and sense of
responsibility towards life in throwing
[th]emselves off a bridge 71 metres (229 feet)
[ab]ove a rampant raging river attached to
[no]thing more than a great rubber band.*

WHEN overseas visitors think of New Zealand, chances are they think of Queenstown. It's the country's premier tourist resort. Annual visitor numbers have topped half a million. A quarter come from New Zealand, the rest from overseas, mainly from Australia, Japan, the United States, the United Kingdom and Germany.

Initially the visitors went there for the same reason as the painters and the photographers, the sheer beauty of the place. They still do. The locals later realised that the district's lakes, mountains and deep river gorges could not only provide the scenery, but the venues for excitement. Adventure tourism was born.

It's a long way from the goldrush days when the Diggers Rest hotel offered the new attraction of rat baiting. Patrons competed to see whose dog could kill the most rats in an enclosed area in a set time. The talk today is not of goldrush but of grand rush and ground rush and adrenalin buzz, all epitomised by bungy jumping.

Queenstown is the home of commercial bungy jumping, also known as paying to throw yourself head first off a bridge or out of a helicopter with a rubber cord tied to your ankles. It dates back to the mid-1980s and two speed skiers, A.J. Hackett and Henry Van Asch, who turned a Melanesian manhood ritual (the men jump from a bamboo tower with fibre ropes tied to their ankles) into a dare-devil craze and then a multi-million dollar international industry.

There are four local sites from which you can turn yourself into a human yo-yo, the historic Kawarau and Skippers suspension bridges, the Ledge near the top of the Skyline Gondola, and a restored pipeline and walkway suspended 102 metres (about 30 storeys) above the Shotover River. If the world's second-highest land-based bungy jump was too tame, you could for a time leap from a helicopter 300 metres above the ground. The first freefall took about 10 seconds before the elastic cord catapulted you back towards the rotor blades. The heli-bungy operation has been put on hold until new safety standards are sorted out. More than a quarter of a million people have taken the 'conventional' bungy plunge locally since the first commercial jumps in 1988.

If you are into airborne activities there are plenty of other options in and around Queenstown. These include skydiving, either solo or tandem with an instructor, and paraflying, which involves being pulled along by a boat while you're attached to a parachute above Lake Wakatipu. There's also solo or tandem hang gliding and paragliding (also called parapenting). These involve

OPPOSITE: COURTESY TOURISM DUNEDIN

JOHN KING

DENIS TODD

OPPOSITE: GILBERT VAN REENEN, CLEAN GREEN IMAGES

running off a mountain while attached to a hang glider or a paraglider, which is a cross between a hang glider and a parachute. A variation involves taking off and landing on snow with skis attached to your feet.

You can also opt for an aerobatics flight in a biplane, or a more relaxed hot air balloon ride, or a scenic flight by helicopter or fixed wing aircraft. Several classic aircraft operate from Queenstown and Wanaka. The hot dry basins and cooler surrounding mountains combine with rising air over the Southern Alps to make Alexandra and Omarama great for gliding. Many world gliding records have been set from both bases and Omarama hosted the 1995 world gliding championships.

The main waterborne activities are jetboating and rafting. Commercial white-water jetboating is another home-grown industry which has since spread around the world. It was developed in Queenstown in the 1960s when the jetboat invented by South Island sheep farmer Bill Hamilton was turned into a tourist activity.

Commercial jetboating is available on the Shotover, Kawarau, Clutha, Dart, Makarora, Wilkin, Waitaki and Taieri Rivers. Most operators delight in taking people on high-speed rides over water a few centimetres deep and within a few centimetres of river boulders and rock walls before finishing with the obligatory 360 degree pin-point turn.

Whitewater rafting on the Shotover River dates back to the early gold miners who used makeshift rafts if they wanted to get out of Skippers Canyon in a hurry. Today's whitewater rafting on the Shotover includes a trip through the Oxenbridge diversion tunnel. It wasn't much use to the Oxenbridge boys, but commercial raft operators have made the most of the wasted labours. Whitewater rafting is also available on the Kawarau, Clutha and Hawea Rivers.

If one adrenalin rush isn't enough, tour operators offer combination trips with names such as Triple Challenge, Triple Bi-Pass, Awesome Foursome and Adrenalin Four. These involve back-to-back mixes of bungy jumps, helicopter flights, jetboat trips and raft rides.

The thrills are not without their spills. Whitewater rafting mishaps in particular have cost several tourists their lives in recent years, and several others have been seriously injured.

Water activities don't end with jetboating, rafting and the more conventional lake cruises available in the district. Different adventures are being introduced all the time. Among the newcomers is whitewater sledging, which involves donning wetsuit and flippers and going down a river while holding onto a float. At the head of Lake Wakatipu, Glenorchy is renown for windsurfing. The mountains act as funnels through the Rees and Dart Valleys to produce one of the fastest windsurfing courses in the world.

On dry land, horse riding, cross country motorcycling and four wheel drive tours are available, and mountain biking is becoming increasingly popular. Four wheel drive vehicles will take you to mining ghost towns, including a ride over the old miners' wagon trail from Arrowtown to Macetown. Bus and four wheel drive trips are also available into the tortuous Skippers Canyon. You can drive in yourself, but it's no place for the novice or the nervous driver.

There are plenty of walks available in the district, from short strolls to independent or guided walks lasting several days. Most are centred on the head of Lake Wakatipu. The Routeburn Track, which starts in Otago, has become so

GILBERT VAN REENEN, CLEAN GREEN IMAGES

popular that numbers have been limited and a booking system introduced. More than 11,000 people walk the Routeburn each year. The Greenstone-Caples and Rees-Dart circuit tracks also start and end near the head of the lake, while the Young-Wilkin circuit track is accessible from Makarora. Guided walks using private huts are available over the Routeburn and Greenstone tracks.

From Queenstown there's little to beat a five to six-hour moonlit walk up Ben Lomond to catch the sunrise over the Remarkables. If you're even fitter and have a couple of thousand dollars to spare, professional mountaineers will escort you to the top of Mount Aspiring.

Walking is just one of the options on part of the former Central Otago branch railway line, which DoC has turned into a rail trail. The 150-kilometre long corridor of track between Middlemarch and Clyde has been ripped up and given over to recreational walking, mountain biking and horse riding. The section between Wingatui near Dunedin and Middlemarch has been retained for an excursion train which takes passengers on half-day tours through the impressive scenery and stone and iron lattice viaducts of the Taieri Gorge.

The Taieri Gorge Railway's colourful refurbished wooden carriages are pulled by modern diesel engines these days. There's no place for diesel on the vintage steam train the Kingston Flyer, or the vintage steam boat the *Earnslaw* on Lake Wakatipu (see Steam, pages 102-105).

In winter, Queenstown and Wanaka are synonymous with skiing, and more recently snowboarding. Coronet Peak and the Remarkables near Queenstown, and Treble Cone and Cardrona near Wanaka, offer some of the best downhill skiing in the Southern Hemisphere. On the Pisa Range across the valley from

GILBERT VAN REENEN, CLEAN GREEN IMAGES

(Top) **Mountain biking is one of Otago's popular new sports.** (Above) **A lone wind-surfer does an 'aerial' on Lake Hawea.** (Opposite Top) **Another bungy challenge at the Kawarau suspension bridge.** (Opposite Lower) **Whitewater rafters negotiate the 'Mother-In-Law' rapid on the Shotover River, near Queenstown.** (Pages 88-89) **Trampers on the world-famous Routeburn Track.**

(Right) **Competitor crosses Price Creek railway viaduct during the biathlon from Ranfurly to Middlemarch, 1996.** (Far Right and Below) **Tourists stretch their legs during the journey from Dunedin to Middlemarch.** (Lower) **Middlemarch: the end of the line.** (Lower Right) **Fast track to the Maniototo, Taieri Gorge Railway.**

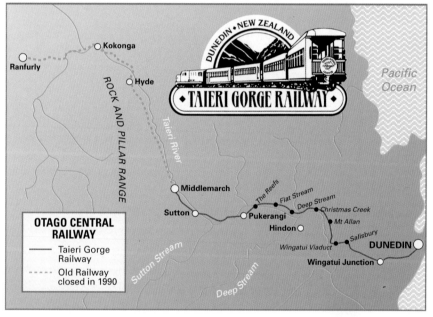

DUNEDIN · NEW ZEALAND

TAIERI GORGE RAILWAY

Kokonga

Ranfurly

Hyde

Pacific Ocean

Taieri River

ROCK AND PILLAR RANGE

Middlemarch

The Reefs

Flat Stream

Deep Stream

Sutton

Pukerangi

Christmas Creek

Mt Allan

Hindon

OTAGO CENTRAL RAILWAY

— Taieri Gorge Railway

···· Old Railway closed in 1990

Salisbury

Wingatui Viaduct

DUNEDIN

Wingatui Junction

Sutton Stream

Deep Stream

MIDDLEMARCH

CHRIS McLENNAN PHOTOGRAPHY

Cardrona, cross country skiing is available at the Waiorau nordic ski area, and in the mountains, heliskiing on virgin snow. In North Otago there's the private Awakino skifield near Kurow, which is open to non-members, and the Ohau skifield on the fringes of the Otago region, while a new ski area is being developed near Glenorchy.

Winter in Central Otago means ice-skating, ice hockey and the ancient Scottish sport of curling. The game is basically bowls on ice played with curling stones. These large round granite stones with goose-neck shaped handles are imported from Scotland. The game is played by two teams of four, each led by a skip. Each player hurls two stones along the ice towards a fixed tee. Team members use straw brooms to quicken the path of any stones which look like they were hurled by someone who didn't have enough porridge for breakfast, or had too much whisky for lunch.

When the weather's right and the water's frozen, teams from throughout the region take part in a two day bonspiel (great match) on the Idaburn Dam near Oturehua. A curlers court is held at the end of the second night, when young players are initiated into the 'brother-hood' of curling during a secret and originally all-male ceremony. Women have been playing the game since the 1890s but it wasn't until 1975 that the Lowburn Club became the first to accept women members.

Increasingly, Queenstown is seen as a destination for tourists and package tours. The locals prefer to take their holidays in quieter places such as Wanaka (except on New Year's Eve) and Alexandra, where they display a tremendous loyalty. Generations of families return to the same town, same camping ground,

(Above) **Snowboarding is now taking off in Otago, while skiing is as popular as ever.** (Opposite) **Coronet Peak ski resort is half an hour's drive from Queenstown.**

OPPOSITE: COURTESY TOURISM DUNEDIN

DENIS TODD

DENIS TODD

(Top) **The ancient Scottish sport of curling is played each year on the frozen Idaburn Dam near Oturehua. (Above) Close-up of the action.**

same site, for the same holiday period year after year. It's an Otago institution.

Bill Parker and his family have been returning to the Glendhu Bay motor camp on the shores of Lake Wanaka since 1958. He has a permanent booking. So do many of his caravaning neighbours. Now his children bring their children to Glendhu Bay each year, to camp alongside his neighbours' children and grandchildren. Bill says his kids had such a great time at the lakeside camp they wanted the same for their kids. In 1995 Glendhu Bay hosted its first wedding. The couple had met at the camp and it seemed the obvious place to get married.

A decade or two ago Otago people outside the Lakes District looked inland with envy from their tourism backwater. What could they possibly offer to compete with the splendour of the southern lakes? It took them a while to appreciate they had a great deal to offer. Dunedin took the resigned Kiwi phrase "It's Alright Here" (usually followed by "I Suppose") and turned it into the confident slogan "It's All Right Here".

First, people on the coast who had taken for granted the wildlife at their back door began to see it as a wonderful natural asset. Dunedin began marketing itself as the wildlife capital of New Zealand.

A host of guided bus and boat tours operate from the city to view wildlife on the Otago Harbour and Peninsula, including the royal albatross, penguins, seals and shags. Further afield, the long neglected little blue penguins which nest on the Oamaru foreshore have been turned into a tourist attraction. In the Catlins, two-day wildlife educational tours are available.

Dunedin and Oamaru also realised they had another asset worth shouting about, in the form of the historic buildings they had been left as a result of their

LEFT AND BELOW: E. OMBLER, CLEAN GREEN IMAGES

declining fortunes. Instead of putting up with taunts about living in Victorian museums, they turned the taunts into a virtue.

Guided bus tours are available of Dunedin's architectural features. Olveston in the city and Larnach Castle on the peninsula are both open to the public, as is the first home built by James Fletcher. The Broad Bay house is a classic Kiwi double bay return verandah villa built in heart rimu.

Back in Dunedin you can walk or drive up Baldwin Street, listed in the *Guinness Book Of Records* as the steepest street in the world. Some people actually run up during the annual Baldwin Street Gutbuster held as part of Dunedin's Festival Week. At its steepest, the street has a gradient of 1 in 1.266, which tilts it at an angle of 38 degrees.

For many visitors, Dunedin is not penguins and palatial mansions, but Cadbury's chocolate, Speights beer and Wilson's whisky. Each of the Dunedin firms offers popular guided tours of their premises. About 18,000 people a year go through the Cadbury's factory. Free sampling is included in each tour, so it's not a good idea to do all three on the same day.

Oamaru meanwhile has turned its attention to the largely abandoned area around its port. Through neglect rather than foresight it just happens to contain the most intact precinct of Victorian commercial buildings in New Zealand.

Oamaru's Whitestone Civic Trust is part-way through a 15-year project to restore the historic Harbour-Tyne Street precinct and turn it into a Victorian town at work. One of the first to take up residence has been bookbinder Michael O'Brien. The former Aucklander not only works with traditional methods and materials but plays the part of an Edwardian gentleman to boot.

(Top) **Otago Cavalcaders cross the Old Man Range near Roxburgh in the annual re-enactment of the miners' treks to the Otago goldfields. (Above) Fleur Sullivan, one of the originators of the annual Otago Cavalcade.**

In November, the town hosts its annual Heritage Oamaru celebrations, including a Victorian fete, the National Penny Farthing Cycling Championships and a whitestone handsawing competition. At nearby Weston you can visit Parkside Quarry, the only place in the country still producing limestone building materials.

Otago is also well endowed with more conventional museums. Top of the list is the Otago Museum in Dunedin. It features displays of Maori and Pacific Island art, New Zealand natural history and the hands-on Discovery World. The museum is complemented by the Otago Settlers Museum, which concentrates on social history.

Most towns outside Dunedin have their own museums, reflecting their district's particular history. There are many specialist museums too. Wanaka boasts the New Zealand Fighter Pilots Museum. Most of the planes are in flying condition and star in the Warbirds Over Wanaka airshow every second Easter. Queenstown has a classic motor museum, Tapanui a vintage machinery museum.

One of the largest museums anywhere has to be the Otago Goldfields Park. You need a vehicle and several days to drive around it. The DoC-administered collection of 21 scattered sites represents an impressive cross-section of the province's gold mining history. Included are the formative Gabriels Gully, the extensive dredge tailings at Earnscleugh, the tortured landscape of the Bannockburn sluicings and the deep mine shafts and stamper batteries above Bendigo. The park also embraces the former Chinese mining settlement at Arrowtown, the ghost town of Macetown, and St Bathans, where miners took a 120-metre high hill and turned it into a 69-metre hole, now filled by the Blue Lake.

Fishing and hunting are major attractions for some visitors, particularly from North America. The Greenstone, Caples, Von and Lochy tributaries of Lake Wakatipu offer some of the best rainbow trout fly fishing in the world. Catch and release is gaining in popularity. In the Route Burn and part of the Lochy River it's compulsory. The best trout fishing would be off the jetty at Queenstown, if it wasn't illegal. The monster hand-fed trout are not for catching, but for watching from the jetty or from an underwater observatory.

The Waitaki River is renown for its sea-run quinnat salmon. The annual Waitaki Fishing Contest in March attracts its share of international entrants keen to pull from the fast flowing water salmon weighing 18 kilograms or

IAN DOUGHERTY

(Above) **Bookbinder Michael O'Brien of Oamaru. (Left) Dunedin's Baldwin Street, the steepest street in the world. (Opposite) Foyer of Larnach Castle, Otago Peninsula.**

IAN DOUGHERTY

more. As a result of the release of salmon into Otago Harbour from 1986, hundreds are now caught in the harbour each year, many from wharves within a short walk of the Octagon.

Deerstalking and game bird hunting are also popular in Otago, as is rabbit shooting. People from all over the country converge on Alexandra each year for the Great Easter Bunny Shoot. Shooting parties are allocated blocks and blaze away for 24 hours. In 1997 they took a record toll of more than 24,000 rabbits.

Tourism has been a huge boost to Otago, but there are concerns that the

(Right) **The Otago Settlers Museum, Dunedin.** (Below) **Dining room at Olveston, the historic home which is a mecca for antique lovers visiting Dunedin.** (Opposite Top) **Kawarau Gorge Mining Centre.** (Opposite Lower) **The losers at the annual Alexandra Easter Bunny Shoot.**

steady trickle of tourists of the 1890s has turned into a downpour which threatens to drown the place. Surveys in Queenstown are turning up not just the usual flattering comments about "the beautiful scenery" and "the wide range of things to do", but also that it's "too expensive", "too commercialised".

Similarly the more Mount Aspiring National Park is promoted as a pristine wilderness where people can get away from it all, the less likely it becomes. People end up falling over all the other people trying to get away from it all. It's a dilemma the local tourist industry is still to tackle.

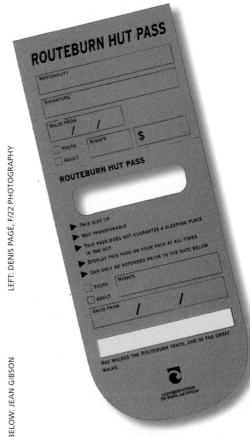

STEAM

A FULL HEAD OF NOSTALGIA

(Above and Opposite) **The TSS *Earnslaw* is a familiar sight on the waters of Lake Wakatipu and has long been one of Queenstown's leading visitor attractions.**

PEOPLE who are older than the TSS *Earnslaw* get a free ride. The response is less than overwhelming, and for good reason, The twin screw steamer was prefabricated in Dunedin, railed to Kingston and launched there on 24 February 1912 (the same day as the launching of the *Titanic*). The qualifying date is actually taken from 18 October, the date the steamer was commissioned. About five people a week take up Fiordland Travel's offer of a free trip.

The "Lady of the Lake" as the vessel is affectionately known, is the last of the steamers to have plied Lake Wakatipu. For a time it looked like she might go the way of the *Titanic*. After half a century of faithful service to the isolated lakeside communities, there was a danger in the 1960s the steamer would be scuttled or scrapped when the roads went in. But her value as a tourist attraction won the day.

The attraction is in the novelty and nostalgia of the propulsion. The 50-metre long vessel is powered by two coal-fired steam engines. Thanks partly to the high quality of the lake water which means minimal rusting, she's believed to be the only surviving coal-fired commercial passenger vessel in the Southern Hemisphere.

Engineer Jack Ellis has been involved with steam boilers all his working life. He's convinced that if the *Earnslaw* was converted to diesel, she would lose her character. What the passengers expect and love is the old fashioned smell of steam and lubricating oil. Being able to see the movement of the exposed engine parts and the fires being stoked and the smoke coming out the stack. Take all that away and she's just another old boat.

Skipper Barry Muldrew talks about the steamer being alive and always warm, thanks to the coal fires. Not a sterile old boat but a real old lady, and a hard working one too, if a bit cranky at times.

Jack Ellis has done some calculations to support the hard work references. He reckons she travels the equivalent distance of a trip from Invercargill to Nelson every week, and once around the Equator every year. Jack and Barry both swear the return trip on the lake is always faster than the way out. They say it might have something to do with the wind or the currents, but they believe it's because the old lady likes to get home and put her feet up.

Nostalgia is not the only appeal. Another is the setting. Lynley Gibson, the first female deck-hand to work on board, talks of the changing moods of the lake from day to day and season to season. In winter, the lake can be like a mirror, reflecting snow from mountain top to water's edge. For the crew, the passengers are an added appeal. Piano player Betty Kingan loves meeting the ever-changing chorus of international visitors who gather around

her for a sing-along. Below decks, stokers Caley Hall and David Waikato are too busy shovelling several tonnes of coal per shift to have much time for scenery. Though it's hard work and it's hot work and the early shift starts at 5am they always find time to explain how the engines function.

At the southern end of Lake Wakatipu, another pair of steam engines are providing a different nostalgia trip. Two vintage steam trains which alternate as the Kingston Flyer travel on the last isolated stretch of the railway line which once carried the Kingston Flyer Express between Kingston and Gore. The Flyer is now restricted to making its scheduled forays a few kilometres across the Otago-Southland border to Fairlight.

The two Pacific Class ABs, the *David McKellar* and the *Greenvale*, are nearly as old as the *Earnslaw*. They were both built in the 1920s. Some of the carriages are even older, dating back as far as 1899. The carriages retain most of their original features, although one concession has been made to changes in etiquette. All the spittoons have been removed.

The Kingston Flyer has a worldwide reputation as a tourist train. It's also something of an international star, with appearances in more than 20 feature films, television programmes and commercials to its credit. In New Zealand it's probably best known for its leading role in the 1972 Crunchie Bar ad, still being shown on television in 1997.

As with the *Earnslaw*, steam is not just a source of motion, but of emotion

T.S.S. EARNSLAW : LADY OF THE LAKE

QUEENSTOWN
BOARDING PASS

Ref No:

No 02703

This ticket is issued only in exchange for pre-paid voucher. No cash value.

FIORDLAND TRAVEL

FTL 50

COURTESY TRANZ RAIL LTD

IAN DOUGHERTY

(Top) **The Kingston Flyer runs twice daily between Kingston and Fairlight from October to April.** (Above) **Driver Russell Glendinning.** (Opposite) **The train is hauled by one of two New Zealand-built steam locomotives carrying 3500 gallons of water in the tender, 4.5 tons of coal and 1000 gallons of water in the boiler.**

for passengers and crew. Engine driver and area manager for Tranz Rail, Russell Glendinning, has been involved with the train since the early 1970s. He says the engines are old and slow, they rattle along, and that's all part of the appeal. For older passengers the Flyer brings back childhood memories. For younger ones it's a taste of an era of which they can only dream.

About three-quarters of the Flyer's passengers are from overseas, many from Japan. Assistant engine driver David Tait has been learning Japanese and making a play for the lucrative bus trade which passes Kingston on the way to and from Queenstown.

There's an edge to the activity. The Flyer faces an uncertain future at Kingston. Having been shunted around different stretches of railway track for a quarter of the century, another move is in the offing. A number of tourist towns have expressed both an interest in acquiring the train and a boast about being able to earn more tourist dollars. One proposal has the Flyer running on a seven-kilometre hillside track overlooking Queenstown.

People in the small lakeside settlement of Kingston have seen the Flyer come and go before. They are not just passionate about the train, but very protective. A Kingston Flyer Promotions group has been formed with the idea that the best way to keep the train in Kingston is to make sure it's popular. Member Archie McDonald, a local cribbie, says he's not the sort of chap who usually gets worked up about issues, but he does about the Kingston Flyer.

OPPOSITE: COURTESY TRANZ RAIL LTD

PEOPLE

"The people are Scotch. They stopped here on their way from home to heaven – thinking they had arrived."

– *Mark Twain, writing in* Following The Equator *of his 1895 visit to Dunedin.*

MOST of the stereotypes about Otago contain at least a grain of truth, including those which portray the place as Little Scotland. The influx of gold miners of various nationalities completely ended any chance of a uniquely Scottish settlement, but the Scottish tradition remains strong, visible and audible, particularly in Dunedin.

The city hosts more than a dozen Scottish dancing and piping groups and Scottish clubs, societies and associations. There's not one, but two rival Scottish heritage councils. It's further proof for some of the old adage that if you leave two Scotsmen together they will either start a clan war or a Caledonian Society.

Dunedin has its own coat of arms, granted to it in 1947 by the King of Arms in Edinburgh. One of the two featured figures is a Scotsman clad in clan Cameron tartan (because Donald Cameron was mayor at the time). The city recently had its own tartan registered at the tartan museum in Comrie in Scotland.

Each March Dunedin hosts Scottish Week, featuring the Queen o' the Heather

(Below) Statue of Scottish poet Robert Burns, The Octagon, Dunedin. St Paul's Cathedral in the background. (Right) Scarecrow Day is another of the many colourful events for which Dunedin's Festival Week has become famous. (Overleaf) The Dunedin haggis ceremony is celebrated in style.

(Opposite Top) **Barracouta curing, Otago Heads (from** *Illustrated New Zealander* **1867).** (Opposite Lower) **1910 photograph of the original Routeburn Flats Hut, on the Routeburn Track.** (Left) **Foreign students studying English at the Otago Language Centre.** (Below) **Craftsman at Portobello Hen Store.** (Lower) **Jetboat driver on the Shotover River.**

contest. The week includes Otago's anniversary day which marks the arrival of the first ship-load of migrants for the new settlement in 1848. Dunedin and Queenstown both have Scottish shops, where you can buy anything from tartan knickers and hand-sewn kilts to clan crested mugs and sporran flasks. A haggis ceremony is another of Dunedin's tourist attractions.

At the heart of the city is a statue not of some politician or soldier, but of the Scottish poet Robbie Burns, whose birthday is celebrated each January by the Dunedin Burns Club. The poet was long dead before anyone had thought of Otago, but he had family connections. He was the uncle of one of the settlement's founders. The statue in the Octagon was unveiled in 1887. A local wag was quick to point out that the bard was sitting with his back to the church (the Anglican Cathedral) and facing the pub (the former Oban Hotel). Today he faces a pub and a wine bar.

The Scottish influence is also evident in religious affiliations. Presbyterians dominate. At 51,000 in the 1996 census, they were easily the largest single group in Otago, far outnumbering the 21,000 Anglicans and a similar number of Catholics.

The other figure in Dunedin's coat of arms represents a neglected and almost forgotten Otago tradition. The figure is a Maori chief wearing a korowai or waist mat.

The relative decline that was Otago's lot for most of the 20th century was something local Kai Tahu knew only too well. The southern Maori population had never been more than a few thousand. By 1844, measles, influenza, small-pox, scarlet fever, typhoid and T.B. had reduced the Maori population of Otago to a few hundred. They and their descendants were largely sidelined.

The 1980s saw a resurgence of Maori culture and moves towards social and economic advancement. A new generation began to re-learn the language and cultural skills. A sign of the revival came with the opening of the Araiteuru urban marae in Dunedin to complement the tribal marae at Moeraki, Puketeraki near Karitane and Otakou.

The revival has been tied to Kai Tahu treaty claims. In Otago there were no land wars and consequent land confiscations, but injustices did take place, particularly in the Crown's failure to provide adequate reserves. The Kai Tahu claims date back to 1849, when the government was first petitioned about the lack of reserves. It's been described as the largest and longest-running legal dispute in the country's history and the longest-running claim of its type in the world.

The Maori population of Otago remains small. The 1996 census recorded 11,000 people of Maori descent, or 6 percent of the Otago region's population. That's the lowest proportion of any region in the country and fewer than 2 percent of New Zealand's total Maori population. Despite the low numbers, the recent settlement of the Treaty claims means Kai Tahu will be an important player in the Otago economy, as major landowner, investor and tourist operator.

In addition to Otago's Scottish and Maori traditions, significant contributions have come from the English, Irish, Chinese and Lebanese communities since the 19th century, and the Dutch and Pacific Island communities in the 20th century. Increasingly Otago, like the rest of the country, is looking to Asia. As a sign of the times, Dunedin now has three sister cities. Edinburgh has been joined by Otaru in Japan and Shanghai in China.

As for the other stereotypes about Otago, there's some truth in them too. There's a belief, for example, that Otago folk are friendlier and more easy going that people further north. The experience of Aucklanders who have migrated against the tide supports the view, although it's probably as much to do with size of population as with nature of people. Small town North Island people are probably just as friendly and relaxed as people in small town Otago, people in Hamilton or Palmerston North just as friendly and relaxed as people in Dunedin.

It's the same story with another popular belief about the south being safer than the north. It's true that Auckland has more crime than Dunedin, but again it's not a fair comparison. And it's idealised nonsense to suggest that most people in Otago still leave the doors to their homes unlocked and their car keys in the ignition.

(Below) **Asian cooking demonstration at the Dunedin festival.** (Lower) **A family affair: Jesse James T-shirt Company.** (Opposite) **Student teacher at Dunedin's College of Education.**

One stereotype which grew out of Otago's Scottish roots has much more validity, that the people are more canny and puritanical. Shopkeepers will tell you that Otago people are more likely to pay cash, less likely to ask for credit, than people further north. There's still a belief that you don't spend what you haven't already earned. Otago people are also less likely to flaunt their wealth in posh houses and flash cars and fast boats. Skiting goes against the grain in the south, at least when it comes to material possessions.

That puritan ethic also includes a wider feeling that people in Otago are more decent and more moral and more virtuous. Deprived of their former place at the top of the economic pile, they have not been slow to look for superiority and solace in such notions.

The often repeated phrase "down south" is accepted by locals as far as geography goes, but morally they tend to regard the north as down. It's an interesting phenomenon. When Otago people think of Auckland, they think of crime and overcrowding and racial strife and decadent lifestyles on borrowed money. When Aucklanders think of Otago, they are just as likely to think of snow-capped mountains and shimmering lakes.

Otago views on the north are underpinned by a feeling that Otago in particular and the South Island in general have been hard done by. A smaller population has meant that whereas the south produces more than its fair share of the nation's wealth, it has comparatively little say over the country's future. The prosperous and powerful North Island consumes the goods and calls the shots.

The feeling is not new. Such lingering resentment came to a head with the Dunedin-based South Island Movement in the late 1970s and early 1980s.

Opinions ranged from the need for the South Island to have a greater say over its own destiny, to calls for complete secession.

The debate focused on decisions to build a dam at Clyde and to install a second Cook Strait cable to transfer more South Island power north. In the 1950s most people had welcomed hydro-electric dams. By the 1970s they were beginning to realise that after construction, Otago benefited very little. The catch-cry was "cut the cable", and let the North Island drift away. With the advantage of hindsight, it was easy to conclude that when in Maori mythology Maui fished up the North Island from his South Island canoe, he should have thrown it back.

The resentment continues. One of the flood of letters to the editor of the *Otago Daily Times* against the proposed Tuapeka dam contained the following:

> That the good people of Otago should allow these apartment-dwelling, market-driven, shiny-bottomed suits from the far-flung north to build a wall and make yet another puddle in our hinterland, well it is inconceivable. ... Do not let these people get away with it again. They are not our people, they follow a different road, a road paved with dollar bills, drawn on our account.
>
> Murray McLachlan, *Otago Daily Times*, 22 February 1995.

If you can generalise about a group as diverse as the people of Otago, there are a few further stereotypes which tend to ring truer than most. First they are a very loyal bunch.

When Otago swimming coach Duncan Laing was excluded from a national

(Opposite Top) **Banjo player at the Autumn Festival, Arrowtown.** (Opposite Lower) **Olympics Day at Tahuna School, Dunedin, 1996.** (Below) **Otago University Zoology researchers nursing a sick shearwater.** (Lower) **Take A Kid Fishing Day, Lake Dunstan.**

DENIS PAGÉ, F/22 PHOTOGRAPHY

GILBERT VAN REENEN, CLEAN GREEN IMAGES

JONATHAN CAMERON PHOTOGRAPHY

(Right) **The Otago Settlers Museum is a treasury of the province's rich cultural history. This collectible plastics exhibition (featuring Janet De Watt) has been one of its more unusual shows.** (Below) **Artist Nicola Jackson (1994 Frances Hodgkins Fellow) taught herself the craft of dollmaking for her 'Exhibiting Tendancies' at the Dunedin Public Art Gallery in 1995.** (Lower) **Dunedin is more famous for its bands than its nightlife, but the city has colourful performers such as Deadman, sound technician, musician and fire-eater extraordinaire.**

JONATHAN CAMERON PHOTOGRAPHY

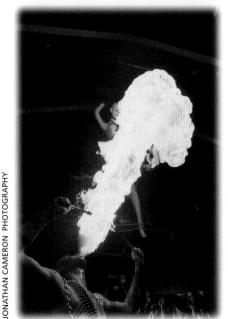

JONATHAN CAMERON PHOTOGRAPHY

coaching squad to travel overseas in preparation for the 1996 Atlanta Olympics, there was a public outcry. The locals couldn't believe that the country's best swimming coach (and the coach of its best-ever swimmer, Danyon Loader) wouldn't be going with the team. They immediately launched a fundraising appeal to enable him to pay his own way, until the northern swimming officials backed down and added him to the coaching squad.

That loyalty doesn't exclude criticism. Otago people can be at the same time highly critical of one another and fiercely loyal in the face of outside criticism.

After Laurie Mains had been appointed All Black rugby coach, his harshest critics came from among the people of his home province, when they were talking amongst themselves. If anyone outside the province dared criticise him, the same people were his most loyal supporters and strongest defenders. There was no hypocrisy involved. That's just the way things are in some families.

The second stereotype which tends to ring truer than most is the one which characterises Otago people as very parochial about their particular patch. Indeed Otago folk have a long and noble history of internal squabbling.

When early politician Vincent Pyke supported Clyde as the district's administrative centre, the people of Cromwell hanged an effigy of him in the town and then threw it into the Clutha River. Naseby has never forgiven Ranfurly for upstaging it as the main town in the Maniototo. People in Wanaka continue to eye Queenstown with suspicion. Some favour completely breaking their ties with the resort and joining the Alexandra-based Central Otago District Council.

The parochialism has its lighter side. This was admirably illustrated by Bob Mitchell, a true blue Oamaruvian who in 1889 published "A Trip Down South" in a collection of his writings entitled *Rhymes And Rambles*.

I've been out through Green Island,
And your boasted Taieri Plain;
Tell me not of homesteads, smiling,
And your fields of waving grain.

I've been to cold Waihola,
And to Tokomairiro too,

DENIS PAGÉ, F/22 PHOTOGRAPHY

(Left) **Trevor Meikle and his dog, Roseberry Farm, Oamaru.** (Below) **A cricket supporter hoists the Otago colours at Alexandra, New Year's Day.**

JONATHAN CAMERON PHOTOGRAPHY

You're only small potatoes
When compared to Oamaru.

I've been as far as Tuapeka,
And the Tapanui Flat,
Mount Benger, and the Beaumont,
And I didn't think much of that.

Through Crookston and the Moa Flat,
The Bend called the Horse Shoe,
It is all barren, bleak, and gloomy,
When compared to Oamaru.

I've been right down through Kelso,
As far as Waipahi,
To own a freehold farm there
I wouldn't sing "Jean McFee".

For your Clinton and the Clutha,
On the banks of Molyneux
I would not swap an acre
Of the farms round Oamaru.

Whereas the parochialism is often at the expense of the neighbour's patch, it is never to the detriment of the province. That's because above all other traits, Otago people are very proud when it comes to their common home. "Pride of the South" is more than just a catchy slogan for the local brewery. For Otago people from the Waitaki to the Catlins, Auckland to London, it taps into an abiding feeling they have for their province, its beauty, its people, its history and its contribution to New Zealand.

Alexandra
Central Otago Visitor Information Centre
22 Centennial Ave, PO Box 56
Ph (03) 488-9515, Fx (03) 448-9516

Arrowtown
Lakes District Museum Information Centre
49 Buckingham St, Ph/Fx (03) 442-1824

Balclutha
Clutha Information Centre
4 Clyde St, PO Box 25
Ph (03) 418-0388, Fx (03) 418-1877

Clyde
Clyde Hydro Information Centre
Visitor Centre Cnr Blyth & Fraser Sts
PO Box 25
Ph (03) 448-9642, Fx (03) 449-2052

Cromwell
Cromwell & Districts Information Centre
47 The Mall, PO Box 2
Ph (03) 445-0212, Fx (03) 445-1649

Dunedin
Dunedin Visitor Centre
48 The Octagon, PO Box 5457
Ph (03) 474-3300, Fx (03) 474-3311

Glenorchy
Department Of Conservation Visitor Centre
Cnr Mull & Oban Sts, PO Box 2
Ph (03) 442-9937, Fx (03) 442-9938

Kurow
Kurow Community Information Centre
45 Bledisloe St, Ph/Fx (03) 436-0812

Lawrence
Lawrence Information Centre
17 Ross Place, PO Box 10
Ph/Fx (03) 485-9222

Makarora
Department Of Conservation Visitor Centre
State Highway 6, Pvt Bag Via Wanaka
Ph/Fx (03) 443-8365

Milton
Milltown Project Board Information Centre
124 Union St. Ph (03) 417-8109, Fx (03) 417-8332

Naseby
Naseby Forest Visitor Centre
Derwent St, PO Box 16
Ph (03) 444-9995, Fx (03) 444-9909

Oamaru
Oamaru Visitor Centre
1 Thames St, Pvt Bag 500-58
Ph (03) 434-1656, Fx (03) 434-1657

Omarama
Omarama Information Centre
36 Chainhill Highway, Ph (03) 438-9610

Otematata
Benmore Hydro Information Centre
Benmore Power Station, Pvt Bag 950 Twizel
Ph (03) 438-7848

Owaka
Catlins Information Centre
Main Road, Ph (03) 415-8371
Department Of Conservation Visitor Centre
20 Ryley St, Ph/Fx (03) 415-8341

Queenstown
Queenstown Travel & Visitor Centre
Cnr Shotover & Camp Sts, PO Box 253
Ph (03) 442-4100, Fx (03) 442-8907
Department Of Conservation Visitor Centre
37 Shotover St, PO Box 811
Ph (03) 442-7933, Fx (03) 442-7932

Ranfurly
Maniototo Information & Resource Centre
Charlemont St East
Ph (03) 444-9719, Fx (03) 444-9166

Tapanui
Tapanui Information Centre
Suffolk St
Ph (03) 204-8199, Fx (03) 204-8302

Wanaka
Wanaka Visitor Information
Ardmore St, PO Box 147
Ph (03) 443-1233, Fx (03) 443-9238
Department Of Conservation Visitor Centre
Ardmore St, PO Box 93
Ph (03) 443-7660, Fx (03) 443-8776

SUGGESTED READING

Anderson, Atholl, *When All The Moa Ovens Grew Cold, Nine Centuries Of Changing Fortunes For The Southern Maori*, Otago Heritage Books, Dunedin, 1983.

Bower, Hilary, *NZ Guides, Queenstown, Wanaka And Central Otago*, G.P. Books, Wellington, 1989.

Dacker, Bill, *Te Mamae Me Te Aroha, The Pain And The Love, A History Of Kai Tahu Whanui In Otago, 1844-1994*, University Of Otago Press/Dunedin City Council, Dunedin, 1994.

Dann, Christine & Peat, Neville, *NZ Guides, Dunedin, North And South Otago*, G.P. Books, Wellington, 1989.

Olssen, Erik, *A History Of Otago*, John McIndoe, Dunedin, 1984.

Peat, Neville, *Land Aspiring, The Story Of Mount Aspiring National Park*, Craig Potton Publishing, Nelson, 1994.

Pope, Diana & Jeremy, *Mobil New Zealand Travel Guide, South Island, Stewart Island And The Chatham Islands*, Reed Books, Auckland, Seventh Revised Edition 1995.

January
Catlins Woodstock, Tawanui.
Glenorchy Races.

February
Dunedin Festival Week.
Hoiho chicks go to sea.

March
Dunedin Scottish Week.
Waitaki Salmon Fishing Contest.

April
Alexandra Easter Bunny Shoot.
Arrowtown Autumn Festival.

May
Otago University Capping Week.
Wordstruck Festival of New
Zealand Writing, Dunedin.
24-Hour Book Sale, Dunedin.

June
Brass Monkey Rally, Oturehua.

July
Queenstown Winter Festival.

August
Wanaka Snowfest.

September
Alexandra Blossom Festival.
Young albatross leave Taiaroa
Head.

October
Rhododendron Week, Dunedin.

November
Otago Goldfields Cavalcade.
Heritage Oamaru Celebrations.

December
Whare Flat Folk Festival.

POSTMARKS FROM OTAGO

PHOTOGRAPHS: IAN DOUGHERTY